Understanding *the* GOSPELS

Understanding *the* GOSPELS

VICENTE BALAGUER
(Editor)

EUNSA
Ediciones Universidad de Navarra, S.A.
Pamplona

Scepter

ISBN: 978-1-59417-071-3

CONTENTS

Chapter 3

Chapter 4

Chapter 5

Chapter 6

Chapter 8

Chapter 9

Chapter 10

Introduction

Vicente Balaguer

These pages provide a short course aimed at bringing the reader up to date regarding the Gospels. The contents were originally designed as an oral presentation that would provide orientation for subsequent lectures by listeners. The course is arranged in ten chapters. After this Introduction, the following material is covered:

The first three chapters concern the formation of the Gospels. They cover the process that occurred from Christ's command to his apostles to preach the Good News (cf. Mk 16:15) to the writing of each of the Gospels in its present form (cf. Lk 1:1–4).

The next four chapters point out the most important characteristics of the Evangelists: Matthew, Mark, Luke, and John. Stylistic features proper to each Evangelist are noted that can help us better understand the image of Christ they present.

Last come three chapters that examine some aspects of the Gospel's contents. These final chapters use scriptural texts to illustrate points in the preceding chapters.

We believe this approach corresponds to the emphases of contemporary research on the Gospels, while at the same time respecting what is said in Vatican Council II's dogmatic constitution *Dei Verbum,* no. 18, which affirms the inspiration of the sacred texts, their historicity, and their relevance as a basis for faith in Christ.

[A]mong all the inspired writings, even among those of the New Testament, the Gospels have a special place, and rightly so, because they are our principal source for the life and teaching of the Incarnate Word, our Savior. The Church has always and everywhere maintained, and continues to maintain, the apostolic origin of the four Gospels. The apostles preached, as Christ had charged them to do, and then, under the inspiration of the Holy Spirit, they and others of the apostolic age handed on to us in writing the same message they had preached, the foundation of our faith: the fourfold Gospel, according to Matthew, Mark, Luke, and John.

WHY THESE TOPICS AND NOT OTHERS?

Each chapter of this book answers, or attempts to answer, a timely question. Fundamental to all is the question: How can one read and understand the Gospels now?

Clearly a Catholic reads the Gospels as historic testimonies to the life and work of Jesus. This is how they were and are read in the Church and in the Tradition of the Church. In this we are one with the great Tradition—with the approach taken, for example, by St. Augustine or St. Thomas Aquinas.

But even though we profess the same faith as the Fathers and Doctors of the Church and take their understanding of Scripture as a guide for our own, our situation and theirs are in some ways quite different. Origen had to respond to Celsus, who affirmed that the accounts of miracles were fraudulent and the Gospels contradicted one another. The educated reader today must respond to the suspicions raised by rationalism, which affirms that the Evangelists did not recount Jesus' actual words and deeds, but presented a kind of metaphorical, mythological picture which the early Christian community then passed on. The Gospels, it is said, do not give us the Jesus of history but the Christ of faith.

It could be said that Catholic research into the Gospels in the twentieth century sought above all to show that this distinction is not that between opposed realities but complementary ones: attentive, rational, methodical study of the circumstances of the early Christian community and the Gospels leads to the conclusion that the Jesus of history is the same as the Christ of faith. Along the way, this research also has led to a better understanding of the Gospels. We shall discuss these matters at length in the pages that follow.

THE THEMES THAT MAKE IT UP

Chapter one, "The Critical Path," is by Juan Chapa, professor of the Origins of Christianity and the New Testament in the University of Navarre's School of Theology. Its timeliness arises from a noteworthy fact. In the last ten or fifteen years many books have appeared that could be generally described as "Lives of Jesus." Some have aimed to shock or to become best-sellers. But others are the work of prestigious Catholic scholars like Joachim Gnilka, Jose Maria Casciaro, John P. Meier, Rudolf Schnackenburg, R. Penna, Raymond Brown, Armand Puig, etc.—or of Protestants—G. Thiessen, J. Schlosser, B. Witherington, etc. Based on a thoughtful examination of the sources, these writers have sought to present a life of Christ that reflects the Gospels and other documents of the time.

True, at times one finds here a certain arbitrariness in deciding what to attribute to Jesus and what to the early Christian community, and on this basis some omit important aspects of the overall picture which they choose to deem inadmissible. The point here, however, is that books like this would have been virtually unthinkable from about 1960 to 1990. The recent lives of Jesus written by specialists show that we have reached a positive moment in research into the Gospels and the life of Jesus, when archeology, combined with greater knowledge of Judaism and of the religion and environment of Palestine in the first century point to the historical verification of what the Gospels say.

To understand this development we need to consider the course of scholarly research on Jesus and the Gospels in the last two centuries. At the end of the eighteenth century the received Tradition was placed in doubt, and people then undertook to rewrite the story of Jesus. In the second period, during the first half of the twentieth century, the possibility of knowing about Jesus with certainty was called into question, and there was doubt whether a "Life of Jesus" could be written. Now—the present moment— that again appears possible.

The chapter will consider two issues in particular: the phases through which research on Jesus has passed in recent centuries; and the criteria of research used to demonstrate the historicity of the Gospels.

In the next chapter, "The Gospels: History and Teaching," I undertake to sum up the positive results of the critical research just described. It has been shown rather clearly that the Gospels must be read just as they are—not only accounts of Jesus, but also a proclamation about Jesus Christ according to the witness of the apostolic preaching. They describe the deeds and words of Jesus while also providing teaching, cat-echesis. They contain teaching inasmuch as they reproduce the preaching of the apostles, which they were obviously trying to spread, along with the memory of Jesus Christ and his actions.

While reading a Gospel passage, someone may ask, "Are Gospel narratives history with doctrine, doctrine dressed in history, or plain history?" As an example, consider the account of the blind man of Bethsaida, as related by St. Mark (Mk 8:22–26). More than once we have heard it said in preaching or have read in a commentary that this episode, coming immediately before the confession of St. Peter at

Caesarea Philippi (Mk 8:23), traces the apostle's faith journey from his first meeting with our Lord up to the time of his confessing him to be the Messiah. First he sees nothing, then he sees something (Mk 8:23)—i.e., men who look like trees walking (Mk 8:24)—and finally he sees everything perfectly, even things far away (Mk 8:25). Typically, the homilist then adds that this is the path followed not just by Peter but by every Christian.

Virtually the whole of the synoptic Gospels receives this treatment. The narrative of the Last Supper in the first two Gospels seems more like the texts of the consecration in the Eucharistic Prayers than a description of events as recalled by any of the twelve apostles. Are the Gospels then an abbreviated report or a catechesis—history, teaching, or both?

Some of these questions are answered in part in chapter one. Chapter two focuses on just one question: what truth about Jesus and the preaching of the apostles is present in the Gospel narratives? This was the chief point investigated and discussed by biblical scholars up to the Second Vatican Council. *Dei Verbum*, no. 19 sums up an instruction of the Pontifical Biblical Commission that remains a basis for studying and reading the Gospels. Guided by that document, I attempt to show that the Gospels are both history and doctrine, and have been such from the beginning. They are faithful to the preaching of the apostles, and the preaching of the apostles is faithful to what Christ said and did.

The third chapter, "Methodologies," is by Juan Luis Caballero, professor of New Testament Studies in the University of Navarre's School of Theology. It complements the two preceding chapters.

In the Church, the Gospels have always been studied closely to determine what it was the Holy Spirit wanted conveyed. For this purpose use has ordinarily been made of techniques used in the human sciences. During the past century, as we have seen, attention has been directed to the formation of the Gospels with two methodological models used especially: form criticism and redaction criticism.

Form criticism may be the more relevant of the two. When reading the Gospels, we observe that, especially when dealing with the public life of Christ, the narrative often seems more like a set of slides than a film. Often, too, scenes seem to be presented according to pre-arranged schemata. So, for instance, accounts of calling by Jesus almost always contain the same or similar actions and words.

Thus the calling of Peter: "As he walked by the Sea of Galilee, he saw two brothers, Simon who is called Peter and Andrew his brother, casting a net into the sea; for they were fishermen. And he said to them, 'Follow me, and I will make you fishers of men.' Immediately they left their nets and followed him" (Mt 4:18–20). Jesus passes by, sees some men, calls them to follow him, and they drop what they are doing and follow him. From the other Gospels, we know that Peter had encountered Jesus before this (cf. Jn 1:43). Here, however, the narrative presents a kind of sketch of what following Christ ought to be like: Feeling oneself called, one should leave everything and follow Jesus. The call of Matthew (Mt 8:9), the call of the rich young man (Mt 19:16–22), and other episodes present the same basic picture. And, in their own ways, this also is the case with passages that deal with other matters, such as Jesus' controversies with the Pharisees.

Form criticism studies these ways of structuring the various narratives that make up the Gospel and tries to determine at what point in apostolic preaching (before the Gospel's were written down) the various schemata used in these accounts may have developed. Clearly, for example, the controversies centering on Sabbath observance would have been hard to describe in a Roman or Greek environment without contact with Jews.

Redaction criticism or narrative analysis, on the other hand, studies how these brief passages are assembled into the continuous narrative of the Gospel. It also seeks the meaning of each passage in the narrative as a whole.

After these first three chapters, the four that follow—by Juan Luis Caballero, Juan Chapa, and myself—consider the four Gospels: Matthew, Mark, Luke, and John. A basic knowledge of the Gospels is assumed. The chapters adopt a traditional structure—author of the Gospel, circumstances of composition, principal characteristics, etc.—to make two basic points.

First, the Evangelists did not say everything they knew. They confined themselves to what appeared relevant to them at the moment. The final verse of the fourth Gospel says: "But there are also many other things which Jesus did; were every one of them to be written, I suppose that the world itself could not contain the books that would be written" (Jn 21:25).

Each Evangelist selected from the material at his disposal and composed his Gospel with a certain purpose in mind. This purpose or orientation depended on two factors: what he had heard and seen or been told by others who were there; and the circumstances of the people for whom he was writing. Here we try to show how the Evangelists were faithful to the Tradition they received (if they were not firsthand witnesses themselves) while at the same time using these events to provide a catechesis for the intended audience.

Second, we take as axiomatic the truism of modern literary criticism that a text's form is a part of the content it transmits—the medium is the message, or at least a good part of it. Even an Evangelist's style can shed light on the essence of his message.

While this way of proceeding has some disadvantages, it has at least two important advantages. One advantage is that this approach helps someone reading the Gospels to better understand what is read. The other is that it elucidates the form that the doctrinal content of each Gospel takes. Rather than using Scripture as a proof of doctrine, doctrine in this way is understood from within.

For example, each of the three synoptics shows Jesus Christ as truly God and man, but each does so in its own way. In Mark, the humanity of Jesus is shown by vivid descriptions of his human sentiments: he is sad, he rejoices, he shows fear, he loves, he praises, etc. In Matthew, Jesus' humanity is illustrated by showing him as a teacher, patiently instructing his disciples.

Chapter eight, "Some Examples," is the work of Juan Luis Caballero. Certain New Testament texts are analyzed in light of what has already been said. The process of establishing their historicity is shown: their doctrinal content is spelled out, and their special features corresponding to particular audiences are identified.

The two final chapters address two kinds of content present in the Gospels. "The Miracles of Jesus" is by Juan Chapa, "The Preaching of Jesus" by Francisco Varo, a professor of Old Testament and History of Judaism in the School of Theology at the University of Navarre. By examining these themes—miracles and teaching—and comparing them with the circumstances of that day, the figure of Jesus stands out more clearly and the intimate relationship existing among who he was, what he did, and what he was sent to do emerges.

Analysis of the Gospel texts and the historical context makes it evident that Jesus not only performed miracles but moreover, his miracles have a special stamp or character of their own: Jesus acts with authority, and his miracles are at the service of the Kingdom of God that he came to establish. Let us consider both of these features.

1. **Authority.** Every miracle manifests God's action in the world, but Jesus' miracles show that God acts in him and not only through him. In this way he performed amazing deeds by his own authority, so that the Evangelists referred to them as *dynameis*, powers. In comparison to

the miracles of some rabbis, which are also documented, in which God responds to the prayer of the chosen with a cure, Jesus, to repeat, carried out those astonishing works by his own authority. The centurion of Capernaum grasped this perfectly, and Jesus praised his faith.

> Lord, I am not worthy to have you come under my roof; but only say the word, and my servant will be healed. For I am a man under authority, with soldiers under me; and I say to one, "Go," and he goes, and to another, "Come," and he comes, and to my slave, "Do this," and he does it. (Mt 8:8–9)

The centurion did not need to ask Caesar's permission to give a command to a soldier that he would carry out; he had that authority, granted by Caesar. Jesus did not need to ask God to perform extraordinary deeds, for he himself had that authority from God.

2. **As a manifestation of the Kingdom of God.** The miracle's purpose was not to exalt Jesus nor even primarily to authenticate his words. They are a way of showing that God's Kingdom is already in the world. Precisely for this reason they also have a teaching, revealing aspect. This aspect is clearer in the fourth Gospel, which refers to the miracles not as "powers" but as "signs," but it also can be seen in the synoptics.

Something similar is true of Jesus' preaching. For one who compares its content and manner with the mode of teaching in that day, it has the same effect that it had on the people of Capernaum when they heard Jesus for the first time. "And they were astonished at his teaching, for he taught them as one who had authority, and not as the scribes. . . . What is this? A new teaching! With authority . . ." (Mk 1:22, 27).

It is like this throughout the Gospel. Consider his parables. He uses them to teach, yes, but not as mere paraphrases of familiar doctrine. Rather, they possess a dynamism corresponding to the new content of what is being preached. Jesus used many rhetorical resources, some very daring, such as "Amen, amen (Truly, truly), I say to you . . ." We shall look more closely at these later.

Wonderment at Jesus' way of teaching was not enough, nor was the awe one feels upon encountering human greatness. On a deeper level it was necessary to affirm Jesus as revealer of God. He said as much himself.

> I thank thee, Father, Lord of heaven and earth, that thou hast hidden these things from the wise and understanding and revealed them to babes; yea, Father, for such was thy gracious will. All things have been delivered to me by my Father; and no one knows the son except the Father and no one knows the Father except the Son and anyone to whom the Son chooses to reveal him. (Mt 11:25–27)

Near the end of his narrative, St. John says it was written "that you may believe that Jesus is the Christ, the Son of God, and that believing you may have life in his name" (Jn 20:30–31). This book shares the same purpose: that we may all understand the Gospels better and in this way understand Jesus better.

1

The Critical Path

Juan Chapa

This chapter deals with the path taken by research on the Gospels during the last two centuries. If there is any common thread throughout, it is summed up in the word "critical." The scholarly study of the first four books of the New Testament has been, and is, critical in two senses: first, that it originally rejected or called into question the interpretation of the Gospels received from Tradition and proposed a new description of the historical reality of Jesus constructed by human reason via a historical method; second, that the results of this scholarly work are themselves subject, at least in principle, to criticism inasmuch as it proceeds like the other human sciences.

HISTORY AND FAITH

At the outset we need to be clear about the relationship between faith and history. Words of Cardinal Ratzinger (now Pope Benedict XVI) on the relationship between the Magisterium and exegesis, in a May 10, 2003, address marking the centenary of the Pontifical Biblical Commission, are helpful here. Speaking of the importance of proceeding by the light of true rationality ("If a purely materialistic explanation of reality is presented as the only possible expression of reason, then reason itself is falsely understood"), he turned to the relationship between faith and history.

The opinion that faith as such knows absolutely nothing of historical facts and must leave all of this to historians is Gnosticism: this opinion disembodies the faith and reduces it to pure idea. The reality of events is necessary precisely because the faith is founded on the Bible. . . . *That Jesus—in all that is essential—was effectively who the Gospels reveal him to be to us is not mere historical conjecture, but a fact of faith.* Objections which seek to convince us to the contrary are not the expression of an effective scientific knowledge, but are an arbitrary over-evaluation of the method. What we have learned in the meantime, moreover, is that many questions in their particulars must remain open-ended and be entrusted to [an interpretation conscious of its responsibilities . . .]. Faith and science, Magisterium and exegesis, therefore, are no longer opposed as worlds closed in on themselves. *Faith itself is a way of knowing.* Wanting to set it aside does not produce pure objectivity, but comprises a point of view which excludes a particular perspective while not wanting to take into account the accompanying conditions of the chosen point of view. If one takes into account, however, that the Sacred Scriptures come from God through a subject which lives continually—the pilgrim people of God—then it becomes clear rationally as well that this subject has something to say about the understanding of the book. (Italics added.)

THE NEED FOR HISTORICAL RESEARCH

Although the historical method has often been employed in a biased way, scholarly study of the Gospels not only has produced useful results but cannot be abandoned. Regardless of the difficulties it has caused, probing the historical character of what is narrated in the four Gospels is of vital importance for Christianity. If, say, new evidence made it incontestably certain that Jesus gestured in a certain way when speaking in public or pronounced Aramaic with a particular accent or wore a tunic of a particular color, this would be of interest not only to the historian but to every Christian; for a historical religion is rooted in earthly realities and material things. Separating the Christ of theologians from the Jesus of history would lead us into dangerous error.

Jesus Christ, the incarnate Son of God, was truly man, living and acting in history. As then-Cardinal Ratzinger points out, if he were only an idea or an ideology, our religion would be a kind of gnosticism. Thus, whatever challenge historical studies of the Gospels, including those carried on outside the context of faith, may raise for Christianity, they enrich and fortify the foundations of our faith by increasing our knowledge of the Lord's humanity.

Still, it is important to ensure that historical scholarship does not overstep the boundaries of its own method. It often happens that the conclusions about the Gospels reached by some historians cannot be accepted because they merely reflect what the historians do or don't believe about God and how he acts in the world. In the past and also today, more than one writer has made the mistake of supposing that scholarship can explain the whole experience of revelation. But—to repeat—scientific demonstration of the historical character of the Gospels is not only perfectly legitimate but more necessary than ever today, when the foundations of faith are so often questioned.

It is impossible in a few pages to say all that needs saying about a matter of this importance. A complete treatment of the question must also include considering how the inspiration of the Holy Spirit proceeded in entrusting these texts to the Church. Other chapters address some of these questions. In what follows I examine only two matters: the history of scholarly research on the Gospels and, in summary fashion, the most important criteria used by scholars to show the historical character of many passages.

1. Research on the Historicity of the Gospels

In its Dogmatic Constitution *Dei Verbum*, no. 19, the Second Vatican Council reaffirmed the Church's acceptance of the historicity of the four Gospels. This affirmation is also found in the *Catechism of the Catholic Church*, no. 126. The conciliar text finds its precedent in the Instruction *Sancta Mater Ecclesia* of April 21, 1964, which is entirely dedicated to this question.

This instruction provides some guidelines with respect to the historicity of the Gospels relating to doubts raised in the preceding decades with the emergence of the method of "form criticism" (it will be explained in greater detail in chapter 4). Although this method is now considered passé to a great extent, it caused considerable uneasiness in the years before Vatican II by emphasizing the role of the community in the composition of the Gospels and questioning the historical character of what they relate. To a certain extent, indeed, form criticism was a turning point in the study of the Gospel narratives.

The Antecedents

From the earliest centuries, Christian writers had defended the historicity of the Gospels on two fronts: against enemies of Christianity who rejected the miracles, they appealed to the guarantee of veracity found in the texts; against divergences in the Gospels, they developed concordances. Along with affirming that the doctrine taught in the Gospels was true, they sought to defend the historicity of the events narrated.

Thus for eighteen centuries Christians accepted the historical truth of the Gospels as a given. With the appearance of the Illuminati and the Enlightenment, a new account emerged, especially in Protestant circles, which denied everything supernatural in the texts. The source of this new thinking lay in the way of conceptualizing the relationship between history and theology that had developed since the Reformation.

Before the Lutheran Reformation of the sixteenth century, exegetical studies were carried out exclusively at the service of the Christian faith, under the authority of the Church and the Creed, and within the framework of the canonical books of Scripture. With Luther, that changed. He refused to accept Tradition as a norm for the interpretation of Scripture while taking Scripture as the sole repository of revelation (*sola Scriptura*). In consequence the key to an upright life came to be the correct reading of the Bible. And for that one had to return to the original text as a point of departure for understanding Christianity as it was in its earliest day.

Luther's modus operandi implicitly included two important presuppositions, and these gradually spread throughout the Protestant world. First, the recovery of origins meant the recovery of essence: the primitive form of Christianity is the best form. This pointed to another premise: any "development" in Christianity had to be a falling-off from the ideal. Second, history served as a theological norm for the reform of the Church: primitive Christianity, uncovered via the recovery of Scripture in its original form, would naturally serve as the norm by which to measure and criticize all subsequent forms of Christianity.

Although Luther could not imagine a form of biblical exegesis that placed itself above the faith, he unwittingly introduced a fissure that later became a chasm. The historical-critical approach to the New Testament and Christian origins developed in the eighteenth and nineteenth centuries among German exegetes was strongly influenced by the British Enlightenment critics; but in their peculiar manner of using history as a measure of theology, these authors were direct descendants of Luther. Meantime, too, the struggle of the latter to defend the faith *against* the Church underwent a transformation into a growing struggle for intellectual freedom, for "a more elevated faith," against the "shadowy" dogmas of Christianity advocated by the official establishment. The historical-critical method became an emblem of freedom in this battle, and was more and more placed at the service of radical opposition to the traditions handed down in the Church.

Positivistic Optimism

Given all this, it is not surprising that much of the study of the Gospels by Enlightenment exegetes and historians since the middle of the nineteenth century was corrupted by a historicist outlook. Rather than being true history, say some authors with a decidedly anti-Christian bent, the Gospels are as it were the costume given Jesus by the apostles: a garment made up of myths suited to an ancient pre-scientific era by which they sought to exalt the figure of the founder of Christianity. This was the perspective for the writing of the "lives of Jesus" at the end of the nineteenth century presenting him as a failed messianic pretender, an idealistic dreamer, or, at best a teacher of religion and morality. A highly optimistic historical positivism was then dominant, with a method based on literary criticism of sources.

The supposed goal of this rationalistic critique was the discovery of "neutral sources" that would allow for an objective historical reconstruction divorced from supernatural or miraculous elements. Attention came to be focused on the synoptic Gospels (in these circles the Gospel of John was considered a theological rather than an historical narrative) and especially the Gospel of Mark, which was judged the most "neutral." Mark was held to be the first Gospel, with a simple narrative of the ministry of the Master. But this approach merely established a basis on which the Gospels, Mark included, could be manipulated as each historian chose.

But the optimism did not last long. Scholars found themselves at a dead end with the publication, in 1901, of the work of Wilhelm Wrede (1859–1906) on Mark and the Messianic secret, underlining the fact that Mark's Gospel was not a simple factual narrative either, but the work of an author with his own theological interests. The final blow was delivered by Albert Schweitzer (1875–1965) whose analysis in 1906 of the various lives of Jesus exposed the subjectivity of the historians in discovering their own ethical ideals in their sources. Thus the quest for the "authentic" Jesus in the Gospels concluded in skepticism regarding the historicity of the narratives. Meanwhile, Leo XIII's encyclical *Providentissimus Deus* (1893) provided a solid basis for biblical studies while placing Catholic exegetes on guard against positivistic influences that took any reference to the supernatural order as illusion or myth (cf. no. 21).

Criticism in the First Half of the Twentieth Century

As a result of the scholarship of the late nineteenth century, pessimism was widespread in rationalistic circles of the first half of the twentieth century regarding the historical character of the Gospels. Rudolf Bultmann (1884–1976) had a major role in this development. This exegete from Marburg, Germany, sought to trace the history of the Gospel tradition along lines initiated by a predecessor, Martin Dibelius (1883–1947), using the method called "form history."

In continuity with Dibelius—who held that the Gospels had been assembled from small independent units ("forms"), with the Evangelists supplying the narrative framework—Bultmann believed he had shown the existence of successive dogmatic "layers" built up by the primitive community. Layer by layer, Jesus was vested with Gnostic or Hellenistic forms and became a myth, the myth of the Son of God. Thus the Evangelists are not historically reliable; the Gospel narratives, Bultmann held, presented a mythologized Jesus unrelated to the Jesus who lived in Palestine. But for Bultmann and the authors who followed him, the historical truth of the Gospels did not matter. What was really of interest from their existentialist perspective was not the Jesus who lived in Palestine, but the Christ transmitted in the *kerygma*, the proclamation of faith by the primitive church. What matters in the end is not whether Jesus did this or said that, but what Christ means for me. That Christ of faith is the Christ who saves me; and I have access to him because the Gospels speak to me about him.

This way of thinking radicalized the distinction made by Martin Kähler at the end of the nineteenth century between the historical Jesus and the Christ of faith. But this gives rise to a disassociation that attacks the very foundation of Christian faith. If sin is a historical reality and we do not know what Jesus actually did, what becomes of the Redemption? The Church's faith has always been solid in this respect: the Jesus of history is the Christ of faith. It is hardly a surprise that Pope Pius XII in 1943 published his encyclical *Divino Afflante Spiritu* to challenge these views that presented a grave danger to the faith and to ground biblical studies in faith and Tradition.

The Mid-century Redaction Criticism

Bultmann's work had and still has enormous influence. It largely occasioned the instruction *Sancta Mater Ecclesia*, cited above. But reaction to the method of form history had begun in Protestant circles some years earlier. Some disciples of Bultmann such as Ernest Kässemann, Joachim Jeremias, and Günther Bornkamm understood the dangers implied by their teacher's position and tried to correct the separation he had created between the real events surrounding the Jesus of history and the story told in the Gospels.

Bultmann had used form criticism to discover the circumstances that led to the attribution of various qualities to Jesus. Now his disciples used "redaction criticism" to show how the Evangelists assembled what they had received and proposed it to their readers. In the late 1950s and through the 1960s they developed the criterion of "discontinuity" as a way of affirming the historical character of something contained in the Gospels: Content that cannot be attributed either to Jewish tradition or the primitive community must necessarily come from an extraordinary personality, that is to say, from Jesus.

While this resulted in a return of sorts to the time when people sought the "objective" content of the narratives, the differences were great. In comparison with the anti-theological historicism of the nineteenth century, the theological motives of the Bultmann era were still strong. The aim now was to emphasize the theological meaning of the Gospels as they were proclaimed by the primitive Church.

Present Trends

Even as the method of redaction criticism arose, new historical sources began to appear, especially through the discoveries of Nag-Hammadi and Qumran, together with new models of research. The so-called Scandinavian School with its studies of the Jewish oral tradition and its forms of transmission, research on the behavior and sociological conditions that favor the transmission of texts, and work carried out by Jewish researchers were among the factors that in the 1960s and 1970s helped give a new direction to the study of the Gospels and encouraged a more positive evaluation of their historicity. This trend has been consolidated since the 1980s thanks to more knowledge of the Gospel sources and the Jewish and Hellenistic context of the first century.

Jewish sources. The last few decades have witnessed many discoveries pertaining to Jewish literature and especially intertestamentary literature. These include the Qumran writings, which testify to the pluralism existing in Judaism in the time of Jesus, and the apocrypha of the Old Testament, key works for knowing the Judaism from which arose Christianity on the one hand and rabbinical Judaism on the other hand. These writings show the vitality of the Jewish religion at the time of Jesus, which was much richer than is suggested by a reading of the Gospels that does not take this context into account; and they show, too, the richness and originality of Jesus' teaching as it is found in the Gospels.

One might also mention the rabbinical teaching that, although not written down until around the third century after Christ, is indispensable to a knowledge of the Judaism of the first century, and the *targumim*, translations of the Bible into Aramaean, which shed light on the way those Scriptures were used in that era. Better knowledge of Jewish sources, in general, has offered and continues to offer new, albeit quite modest, contributions. Another new factor from the point of view of historiography is the growing interest in Flavius Josephus and his re-evaluation as an historian. These developments—along with others in other fields to be noted later—are reflected in numerous recent works on the Gospels emphasizing the Jewish character of the narratives.

Greco-Roman sources. Besides this multiplication of Jewish sources, recent years have brought more use of other sources from the Greco-Roman world. These contribute to a better understanding of the Hellenistic cultural influence present in a good part of first-century Palestine that also helped shape the Gospel texts. The study of Greek magical papyruses, for example, has served to illustrate the popular religiosity of the Mediterranean world (e.g., the attitude toward sicknesses, demons, malignant and benign spirits, amulets, etc.). Greco-Roman rhetorical texts (especially the *Progymnasmata* of Theon), reflects many aspects of Hellenistic education and the Greek philosophical schools. They depict a type of education, widely extended throughout the whole Mediterranean area, in which itinerant preachers occupied an important position.

Apocryphal literature. Extra-canonical texts provide another important perspective for the study of the Gospels. They include apocryphal writings of the New Testament era and the codices of Nag-Hammadi, a Gnostic library discovered in Egypt in 1945. Some authors attribute special importance to the apocryphal Gospel of Peter, the Egerton papyrus containing the Gospel of the Cross, the Gospel of Thomas, the Gospel of Philip, and the Apocrypha of John. The picture of Jesus and his teaching found in these Gnostic texts is so distorted as to render their historical value highly problematical. Comparing them with the canonical Gospels does nevertheless indicate the path that the true faith followed; in addition they provide information that cannot be totally ignored regarding Christianity's earliest years.

Archeological discoveries. Finally, certain recent archeological findings illustrating the Gospels' historicity have been incorporated into the discussion. The results of the excavations being carried on in Galilee are of special interest for the insight they provide into this Hellenized region of first-century Palestine.

The new studies of the Gospels have also given rise to new methods of analysis. Joining form criticism and redaction criticism are approaches drawn from literary criticism (structuralism, rhetorical analysis, narrative theology, etc.) and other sciences and perspectives (psychology, feminism). Also important are works that draw upon sociological studies and apply the methods of cultural anthropology to the Gospels.

It is difficult to say what result this new burst of interest in the Gospels' historicity will have considering its many disparate elements. Still, there is general agreement that the content of the Gospels has been situated more securely then before in the Jewish world of first-century Palestine. Not all the researchers think alike; but in general these studies confirm what the Gospels contain. It is once more possible to write a life of Jesus, with the Gospels as its reliable source.

In Summary

The Pontifical Biblical Commission, in *The Interpretation of the Bible in the Church* (1993), evaluated these methods and approaches, noting their contributions and limits. It concluded by urging the continuation of efforts to investigate the Word of God, efforts that cannot be divorced from history: for God's Word became incarnate in a particular time and place, and these must be studied with the help of human sciences. Nevertheless, the aim of exegesis goes beyond analysis; it must contribute to transmission of the content of the inspired writings.

Three fundamental points need to be borne in mind concerning the research on the Gospel carried out in the last two centuries. First, the content of the Gospels has resisted the waves of historical criticism. Second, interpretations of the Gospel narratives often are creations of the researchers that do not correspond to what the Evangelists say. Third, research at times is limited to merely human aspects. The Jesus who results is only an extraordinary teacher, albeit with qualities that transcend the particular historical context. Jesus, however, is more than an extraordinary teacher; he is, St. Peter confessed, the Son of God (Mt 16:16). One comes to say this not by historical research but by a grace of God.

2. Criteria of Historicity

Why has historical research on the Gospels had such varied results? The answer is twofold. Part of it resides in the absence of consensus about which sources to accept as independent and reliable. Since not all the authors have the same point of departure (for example, on the value they assign the Gospel of John or to the apocryphal gospels), it is difficult to reach minimally homogeneous conclusions. Moreover, there is disagreement as well about what method should be used to legitimatize sources, with different methods employing different criteria.

These criteria, usually referred to as "criteria of authenticity" or "criteria of historicity," are proper to historical methodology. Their function is to verify the historicity of what the New Testament or pagan sources relate. Scholarly research fueled by these principles has developed along the following lines.

Indications and Criteria

Some authors call attention to the distinction between criteria and indications. A criterion carries more weight than an indication, with the latter suggesting probabilities but not a certain judgment of historical authenticity. For example, an indication of the historical character of an incident is the presence of neutral details, having no theological connotations: Jesus sleeping on a pillow, an event occurring "near Jericho," etc. Colorful details and vivid narration (e.g., Mark) indicate eyewitness testimony.

But indications are only that. They could be the result of literary technique. Thus a resemblance to fact has little value for historians. By contrast, criteria have intrinsic value of their own, and in combination can have certain and fruitful results. Yet no more then indications do they amount to irrefutable proof, and they are valued differently by different people. Hence the absence of unanimity regarding a number of questions.

The Most Important Criteria

1. In practice, the criterion used most has been that of "discontinuity" (or dissimilitude or distinction). Käsemann, the first to distinguish and apply the criteria of authenticity to the Gospels, established this criterion as the basis of research on historicity. It is generally as follows: something found in a Gospel can be taken as authentic when it corresponds to neither Jewish thinking at that time nor

to ideas peculiar to early Christianity. That is, its historicity probability is stronger to the degree that its content and ideology differ from those of its sources. If Jesus is presented as saying or doing things that do not seem to fit either Palestinian Judaism or the primitive Church, what is reported very likely is authentic: for example, his use of the word "Abba," "Amen" at the beginning of a sentence, his baptism by John, the apostles' defects, expressions like "the Kingdom of God," the "Son of Man," etc.

This criterion of dissimilitude—between the two poles that establish the parameters of Jesus' history, and the primitive Church—is completed by other criteria, whose importance and number vary in the view of different authors. There is no agreement on their designation or the priority among them. Nevertheless, besides discontinuity (also called originality or dual irreducibility), there is a certain consensus in recognizing as major criteria "multiple testimony" (also called cross references), "consistency" (also called congruence or conformity) and "necessary explanation."

2. The criterion of "multiple testimony" is common in the historical sciences. Something is deemed more historically probable if attested to by more than one source, according to the classic formula *testis unus, testis nullus* (one witness is no witness). Applied to the historical figure of Jesus, this implies that something attested to in all the Gospel sources (the synoptics and John) and in the other writings of the New Testament is authentic. For example, Jesus' mercy is an element in all the sources and the most diverse literary forms, and therefore is historically authentic. This criterion is very important in determining the basic outlines of the person, preaching, and activity of Jesus: for instance, his attitude toward the Law, the poor and sinners, his resistance to being embraced as a

messiah-king of a political sort, his activity as a miracle worker, his preaching in parables.

3. The criterion of "consistency" (or "conformity") signifies that material that cannot be established as historical by other criteria may, nevertheless be judged authentic if generally consistent with other credible information. This is especially the case as it pertains to the heart of Jesus' message, the coming of the messianic Kingdom. On this basis one can affirm the historicity of the parables, the beatitudes, the Our Father, etc. Together with "discontinuity," this criterion allows one to situate Jesus in the culture and traditions of his time.

4. "Necessary explanation" is an application of the principle of sufficient reason, derived from law, to the field of history. An explanation that sheds light on a collection of otherwise enigmatic elements and shows how they fit together, without creating greater problems, points to the authenticity of what is related: e.g., the initial success of Jesus' ministry, his activity in Jerusalem, his private instruction of his disciples, etc.

In general, most scholars now explicitly or implicitly employ these four criteria, either as criteria properly so called or as indications. Their functional principles include "difficulty" (sayings or deeds are authentic if they would have disconcerted or created difficulties for the primitive Church: e.g., Mark 13:32, which says Jesus did not know the final day or hour); "rejection and execution," which determines which of Jesus' words and deeds would lead to his violent death as "King of the Jews;" "historical presumption" (does the burden of proof rest on the side of those who deny historicity or those who affirm it—*in dubio pro traditio* or not?); "Aramaic traces," "Palestinian environment," "narrative vividness," "editorial tendency of each Evangelist," "internal intelligibility of the narrative," "varying interpretation and fundamental agreement," etc.

Finally, it must be recognized that many who study the Gospels today do so on the basis of an unstated assumption: the truth of a post-Enlightenment vision of the world according to which something is more historically trustworthy if it does not contradict modern notions of reality. In other words, they operate on the a priori assumption that certain things in the Bible did not happen because *they could not have happened*, regardless of the number of sources, dissimilitude, consistency, and so on.

The historicity of what is narrated in the Gospels can be shown today by the convergence of the most diverse criteria. Despite some dissent, a great part of the Gospel material is indisputable. But something needs to change in the attitude of some historians toward the Gospel texts. Suspicion should give way to a more consistent and rational attitude. The Gospels deserve to be trusted. Finding themselves unable to demonstrate the contrary, these historians should accept the fact that Jesus is the source of the words and deeds collected in those narratives.

3. CONCLUSION

There is a visible continuity throughout these two hundred years of research on the Gospels involving innumerable attempts to present a picture of Jesus as close as possible to the historical reality. The new approach to understanding Scripture arising from the Protestant Reformation and, above all, the secularized, rationalist, and historicist emphasis of the Enlightenment has conditioned studies and continues to exercise a powerful influence. But it does not follow that one should be suspicious toward the historical approach. Discernment and purification, not renunciation, are in order. All efforts to probe the historicity of the Gospels help us to understand God's salvific action in history and escape turning faith into an ideology. And this is a requirement of faith itself.

2

The Gospels
History and Teaching
Vicente Balaguer

This chapter considers two closely related aspects of the Gospels: their historical character and their doctrine and teaching. At first, these questions may seem opposed, since, as noted above, a neutral narrative describing events without drawing conclusions seems to have more historical value than one in which nearly every detail implies a teaching. Moreover, historical narrative looks to the past while an account that proposes to instruct looks to the present. Yet the Evangelists sought to be—and were—both historical and pedagogical. Christian exegesis of recent years has shown (and this is also reflected in certain documents of the Magisterium) that the Gospels are historical, but not in an anecdotical manner, presenting episodes and events of the life of Jesus as a chronicler might have done. The Gospels relate events that truly occurred in the life of Jesus, but from the beginning these episodes have been understood and expressed as doctrine and teaching.

To understand this dimension of the Gospels, it is necessary to bear in mind that what they transmit is the apostolic preaching about Jesus. One might say that the Gospels do not reproduce the preaching of Jesus, but the preaching of the apostles about Jesus' words and deeds. Obviously, in proclaiming *about* Jesus, the apostles also gathered the preaching *of* Jesus. But we must be aware of the apostolic mediation between Jesus and ourselves. The preaching of the apostles, guided by the Holy Spirit, consisted in proclaiming events they witnessed while drawing out their meaning. They communicated what the Master did and taught, but they accompanied this with explanations—explicit or implicit—of what they related.

1. The Gospels as an Ensemble of Narratives

From the literary point of view, the Gospels, especially the synoptic Gospels, are unusual writings. Two things are immediately obvious.

1. Although they present a continuous narrative of Jesus' activity, this normally is done by means of scenes. With the exception of the Passion narrative, the result is more like a carefully organized set of slides than a motion picture.

2. Each of these episodes (or "pericopes" in the terminology of biblical studies) is very rich. The narratives are short and meaningful, with scarcely an unnecessary word. Often, too, each seems in its own way to sum up the whole of the Gospel.

While homilists and commentators sometimes convey this density of meaning, the New Testament texts by themselves are capable of doing that. They were, after all, inspired by the Holy Spirit and concern the actions and words of Jesus himself. Still, someone influenced by rationalist ideas might attribute this richness of context and meaning to the human authors and suspect that the things related did not occur as related: perhaps the Evangelists reshaped some ordinary event as a doctrinal treatise cast in narrative form. Thus many commentaries on the New Testament repeatedly say things like, "Here Mark (or Matthew or Luke) tells a story in order to make the point that . . ."

In reality, all these factors converge in the Gospels: Jesus himself gave his actions profound significance; the Holy

Spirit provided the Church all it needs for its sanctification; and the Spirit used the sacred authors and their narrative talents to instruct the faithful. We shall see all these factors at work in the chapters that follow. Here, instead of dwelling on abstractions, we need now to examine some texts: for example, the curing of the blind Bartimaeus.

> And they came to Jericho; and as he was leaving Jericho with his disciples and a great multitude, Bartimaeus, a blind beggar, the son of Timaeus, was sitting by the roadside. And when he heard that it was Jesus of Nazareth, he began to cry out and say, "Jesus, Son of David, have mercy on me!" And many rebuked him, telling him to be silent; but he cried out all the more, "Son of David, have mercy on me!" And Jesus stopped and said, "Call him." And they called the blind man, saying to him, "Take heart; rise, he is calling you." And throwing off his mantle he sprang up and came to Jesus. And Jesus said to him, "What do you want me to do for you?" And the blind man said to him, "Master, let me receive my sight." And Jesus said to him, "Go your way; your faith has made you well." And immediately he received his sight and followed him on the way. (Mk 10:46–52)

A commentary is likely to say that Mark is here depicting a journey of faith. A man without faith is a *blind man* like Bartimaeus sitting *at the side of the road*—understood as the road of life—at the mercy of others who do not let him express himself. Upon encountering Jesus, he obtains faith by insistently petitioning for it—having begun to see, he sets foot on the path of discipleship. Going further, a commentator may speak of perseverance in prayer, of leaving behind one's mantle—i.e., one's possessions—in order to respond with alacrity to Jesus' call, and so on. There is much pedagogical potential in the text.

But as such an exposition proceeds, someone may begin to suspect that this story is "true" in the same sense as the parables in Luke 15—that is, true to life—but not historically true. Here, he may suppose, is an exemplary story, expressing what it is to have faith in the manner of a narrative.

This false dilemma—between truth and "truth"—is what Catholic exegesis has wrestled with in the last half century. Its aim has been to show how the Gospels, rich in meaning as they are, are at the same time historically trustworthy.

2. The Gospels Recount the Preaching of the Apostles

What has just been said about the Bartimaeus episode is true of many other passages. So, for instance, the account of the institution of the Eucharist (Mt 26:26–29; Mk 14:22–25; Lk 22:19–40), appears more like what happens at Mass now—following the command of Jesus Christ himself (1 Col 11:23–26)—than like the rites of the Paschal meal, which are not described in the account. And so also for Jesus' calling of the apostles and virtually all the rest of the Gospel.

It could not be otherwise. The narratives of the synoptic Gospels are simple, dense, profound, with almost no room for the merely anecdotal. "Many things about Jesus of interest to human curiosity do not figure in the Gospels," says the *Catechism of the Catholic Church* (no. 514). Teaching and doctrine are everywhere present, for the Gospels are not just contemporary chronicles of the life of Jesus. They originate in the apostolic preaching, which in turn is faithful to the meaning of what Jesus said and did.

This is why the narrative has the quality I have called density. Each account is related to precise circumstances of the life of Jesus, but each also expresses the teaching of the apostolic preaching. This conclusion is not only derived from modern research but is a constant theme of the early Fathers of the Church. St. Justin, for example, calls the Gospels *recollections of the apostles*. St. Irenaeus, Clement of Alexandria, and all who spoke about the origins of the Gospels declare their apostolic source. Thus, when they speak of Mark and Luke—the two Evangelists who are not themselves apostles—they insist that they reproduce, respectively, the *preaching of the apostles* Peter and Paul.

The Magisterium of the Church takes account of both the received Tradition and the results of modern historical and literary research in speaking of the formation of the Gospels and of how they should be read and proclaimed. The Pontifical Biblical Commission does this in some detail in the Instruction *Sancta Mater Ecclesia. De Historica Evangeliorum Veritatem* ("The historical truth of the Gospels," April 21, 1964, in AAS 56 [1964] 712–1718), whose most important points are condensed in no. 19 of Vatican II's Dogmatic Constitution *Dei Verbum* (1965). Let us look more closely at this text.

3. THREE STAGES IN THE COMPOSITION OF THE GOSPELS

No. 19 of *Dei Verbum* shows how the Church understands the Gospels and how we should, too. This is the text:

> Holy Mother Church has firmly and with absolute constancy maintained and continues to maintain, that the four Gospels just named, whose historicity she unhesitatingly affirms, faithfully hand on what Jesus, the Son of God, while he lived among men, really did and taught for their eternal salvation, until the day when he was taken up (cf. Acts 1:1–2).
>
> For after the ascension of the Lord, the apostles handed on to their hearers what he had said and done, but with that fuller understanding which they, instructed by the glorious events of Christ and enlightened by the Spirit of truth, now enjoyed.
>
> The sacred authors, in writing the four Gospels, selected certain of the many elements which had been handed on, either orally or already in written form, others

they synthesized or explained with an eye to the situation of the churches, the while sustaining the form of preaching, but always in such a fashion that they have told us the honest truth about Jesus. Whether they relied on their own memory and recollections or on the testimony of those who "from the beginning were eyewitnesses and ministers of the Word," their purpose in writing was that we might know the "truth" concerning the things of which we have been informed (cf. Lk 1:2–4).

The conciliar text is a single paragraph, but here it is broken into three paragraph-like segments to emphasize the division of thought. It makes two main points:

1. The historicity of the Gospels is affirmed unconditionally.

2. It is important to take into consideration what Jesus said, what the apostles preached, and what the Evangelists wrote. The document proceeds from Jesus to the text of the Gospels, but one could also start with the Gospels as compositions of the Evangelists who, in order to write them, drew upon the oral and written traditions found in the apostles' preaching. The latter in turn understood the deeds and sayings of Jesus in the light of Christ's resurrection and under the inspiration of the Holy Spirit.

This explanation of the formation of the Gospels has consequences both for research and for the reading of the texts. It can best be understood by examining each of these three stages in the process by which they came to exist.

The First Stage: The Words and Deeds of Jesus

Dei Verbum says the Evangelists "faithfully hand on what Jesus, the Son of God, while he lived among men, really did and taught for their eternal salvation, until the day when he was taken up." In reading the Gospel, we encounter Jesus and come to understand what he did. The Evangelists depict the time, place, and environment in which he lived, that is, the Jewish milieu of Palestine in the first three decades A.D.

As the last chapter pointed out, the study of archeology, of the Jewish literature of the time, and of other sources helps us understand the Gospels and provides a historic basis for what they relate. It is necessary to establish both the *continuity* and the *discontinuity* between Jesus' words and deeds and his surroundings. Continuity was required for his message to be understood. But discontinuity is reflected in the fact, clear from the texts, that Jesus was conscious of his essential singularity and manifested it.

Some examples will help. The first example concerns the understanding of the Old Testament as expressed in *norms of conduct*. Different Jewish groups—Sadducees, Pharisees, Essenes, etc.—lived these norms very differently in Jesus' day; and it appears that, without going to extremes, he lived them in a manner similar to some Pharisees, who, drawing on oral tradition and exhibiting a zeal to sanctify the whole of life, regulated daily behavior with many rules. There are thousands of examples in the Gospels (cf. Mk 7:1–15). Yet, Jesus *preached* a way of life that often more nearly resembled that of the Sadducees: i.e., observing the Law of God without being suffocated by thousands of small rules as in some Pharisaical traditions. This is sometimes expressed by saying Jesus preached an *aristocratic ethic* (the Sadducees were the aristocratic class) *for all the people*. While such a generalization may leave much to be desired, it does clearly express his personality. In sum, knowing the circumstances in which Jesus lived makes it clear that Jesus' word and deeds were not simply those of a Pharisee or a Sadducee. They can only be explained by his uniqueness and the uniqueness of his mission.

Or consider another example involving manner of argumentation. The Sadducees challenge Jesus concerning the resurrection, using the case of a woman married and widowed by seven brothers in succession (Mt 22:23–33). Jesus defends the reality of the resurrection with on Old Testament passage accepted by the Sadducees, without appealing to the oral tradition typically called into play by the Pharisees. But when arguing with the Pharisees about the plucking of wheat on the Sabbath, he employs their interpretative method.

> At that time Jesus went through the grain fields on the Sabbath; his disciples were hungry, and they began to pluck heads of grain and to eat. But when the Pharisees saw it, they said to him, "Look, your disciples are doing what is not lawful to do on the Sabbath." He said to them, "Have you not read what David did, when he was hungry, and those who were with him: how he entered the house of God and ate the bread of the Presence, which it was not lawful for him to eat nor for those who were with him, but only for the priests? Or have you not read in the law how on the Sabbath the priests in the temple profane the Sabbath, and are guiltless? I tell you, something greater than the temple is here. And if you had known what this means, 'I desire mercy, and not sacrifice,' you would not have condemned the guiltless. For the Son of Man is lord of the Sabbath." (Mt 12:1–8)

Here Jesus uses two examples: David, who ate the bread of the Presence, and the priests, who work on the Sabbath without breaking it. Basically, he is using the first rule for interpreting the law proposed by Rabbi Hillel, one of the most prestigious teachers among the Pharisees of that era. The rule, called *Qal wa-homer*, means in general: "from the lesser to the greater and vice versa" or "a fortiori." Having cited his two examples, Jesus then says that he is greater than the Temple, and in effect that he is greater than David and the priests. Thus questioners were compelled to ask themselves who he really was.

Much more could be said—and will be said later. Here we only repeat that, with the aid of auxiliary sciences, it is possible to attain a true knowledge of Jesus and his preaching. Knowledge of Jesus' time and place helps us understand him and his mission, while also building confidence in what the Gospels say.

Next, the second stage marked out in *Dei Verbum*.

The Second Stage: The Apostolic Preaching

The books of the New Testament, especially the Acts of the Apostles, point to a second very important stage in the history of Christianity, after the Ascension when, as *Dei Verbum* says, "the apostles handed on to their hearers what he had said and done, but with that fuller understanding which they, instructed by the glorious event of Christ's resurrection and enlightened by the Spirit of truth, now enjoyed." This stage also is reflected in the Gospels.

Supposing Jesus' earthly life to have occupied the years 1–30 A.D., this second stage extended from about 30–60 A.D. Instructed by the Holy Spirit and by the light Jesus' resurrection shed on his life, they now understand him better. Moreover, their own dispersal, as recorded in the New Testament, broadens the scope of their activity throughout the Roman Empire.

Start with the first circumstance. After the resurrection, the apostles knew the terminal point of Jesus' earthly life and had a better grasp of what he had done. We get a glimpse of this in the synoptic Gospels, and it often is explicit in the Gospel of St. John. For example:

> Jesus answered them, "Destroy this temple, and in three days I will raise it up." The Jews then said, "It has taken forty-six years to build this temple, and will you raise it up in three days?" But he spoke of the temple of his body. *When therefore he was raised from the dead, his disciples remembered*

that he had said this; and they believed the scripture and the word which Jesus had spoken. (Jn 2:19–22)

This is explicit, but the same thing frequently is implicit in all of the Gospels. So, for instance, the Gospel of St. Luke often speaks of Jesus as the Lord. Then as now, the word "lord" referred to various prominent people, e.g., members of the hereditary nobility; but "Lord" also is a way of speaking of God, without unnecessarily pronouncing his name. In St. Luke, the word lord as applied to Jesus most often is used the second way.

The point is clearer when one considers the episode of Peter's confession in the Gospel of St. Matthew (Mt 16:13–20). Jesus tells Peter that confessing him to be the Son of God was not something natural but a revelation of the Father. Similarly, all the passages affirming the divinity of Jesus in one way or another are clearer in light of the resurrection.

As for the change of context of the apostolic teaching, the first thing that changed was the cultural setting. The preaching of the apostles began in Palestine, but it developed primarily outside Palestine in the territory of the Roman Empire and was directed to Jews and pagans; different forms of argumentation were used with each group. Examples help make this clear.

The controversies with Jews. We know from the Acts of the Apostles and the epistles of St. Paul that the Jewish Christians entered into controversy with Jews who did not become Christians. The Gospels also reflect the situation of those first Christians living among Jewish neighbors. This is especially true of numerous passages in the Gospels of St. Matthew and St. John. In one well-known instance pertaining to the resurrection, Matthew remarks that the fiction about the stealing of the body of Jesus still persists (Mt 28:15); the Evangelist in response to this calumny explains how the false story got started. (St. Augustine, commenting on this passage, echoes

Matthew, saying: "Wicked guile, you present sleeping witnesses? You were really asleep yourself in inventing such nonsense" [*Enarrations on the Psalms,* 63, 15]).

There are many examples. Thus the expression "their synagogues," which appears more than once in the first Gospel. "Beware of men; for they will deliver you up to councils, and flog you in *their synagogues*" (Mt 10:17), could imply that there were Christian synagogues and synagogues that had not yet become such.

Or consider again that grain which was plucked on the Sabbath. Here as elsewhere (Mt 9:13) we find this: "And if you had known what this means, '*I desire mercy, and not sacrifice*,' you would not have condemned the guiltless." This passage from Hosea was very present to Jewish consciousness after the destruction of Jerusalem by Titus in 70 A.D. With no Temple for worship, God's preference for mercy over sacrifice is clear. In the apostolic teaching, therefore, Jesus' teaching may have been recorded with a note of fulfillment; clearly in Matthew it connects with both the life of Jesus and the life of the community in contact with Judaism.

Another example: The episode involving the man born blind, as related by St. John (Jn 9:1–32). When his parents declined to speak for their son, it is said that the Jews "had already agreed that if any one should confess him [Jesus] to be Christ, he was to be put out of the synagogue" (Jn 9:22). After the destruction of the Temple, some Jews decreed the penalty of expulsion from the synagogue for heretics (probably, Jewish Christians). Perhaps then the incident related by St. John looks to both a particular moment in the life of Christ and a later moment in the history of Christian evangelization.

Many other conflicts between Jesus and the Pharisees could be analyzed this same way.

The context of the apostolic mission. It is clear from the New Testament that the apostolic mission occupied much of the energy of Christ's disciples. In Acts, the apostolic preaching to the Jews shows how Jesus was the fulfillment of the Scriptures. From this point of view, it is possible to approach the Gospels with the intention of determining the context to which some teaching of Jesus was being applied. For example, discipleship and its relation to mission provides a context for accounts of Jesus' calls. The narrative of the calling of the first four apostles (Mt 4:18–22; cf. Mk 1:16–20; Lk 5:1–11), could not be more starkly simple:

> As he walked by the Sea of Galilee, he saw two brothers, Simon who is called Peter and Andrew his brother, casting a net into the sea; for they were fishermen. And he said to them, "Follow me, and I will make you fishers of men." Immediately they left their nets and followed him. And going on from there he saw two other brothers, James the son of Zebedee and John his brother, in the boat with Zebedee their father, mending their nets, and he called them. Immediately they left the boat and their father, and followed him.

In St. Matthew and in St. Mark this is the first time these disciples are named. From the Gospels of St. John (Jn 1:35–51) and St. Luke (Lk 4:14–39; 5:1–11) we know that Jesus had contact earlier with these four. But the account in Matthew has a simple pattern: Jesus' call and the immediate response of the disciple. This is easy to commit to memory and effective. Very similar are the accounts of the calling of Matthew (Mt 8:9 and parallel passages), the rich young man (Mt 19:16–22 and parallel passages, though here the first step is a question from the young man), those who wanted to follow Jesus (Lk 9:7–62), etc.

The important point is that the text does not merely recount an anecdote but teaches something about the Lord's call, the response it immediately elicits and the abandonment of one's former preoccupations, etc.

The context of catechesis in the Church. Chapter 18 of St. Matthew, which is very similar to chapter 9 of St. Mark, is sometimes referred to as "the discourse on the Church." It draws together a number of norms for ecclesial life: forgiveness of sins, the handling of sinners who ignore rebukes, and so on. These matters are also mentioned in other places, although indirectly. For example, there is the episode of the paralytic in Capernaum:

> And getting into a boat he crossed over and came to his own city. And behold, they brought to him a paralytic, lying on his bed; and when Jesus saw their faith he said to the paralytic, "Take heart, my son; your sins are forgiven." And behold, some of the scribes said to themselves, "This man is blaspheming." But Jesus, knowing their thoughts, said, "Why do you think evil in your hearts? For which is easier, to say, 'Your sins are forgiven,' or to say, 'Rise and walk?' But that you may know that the Son of man has authority on earth to forgive sins"—he then said to the paralytic—"Rise, take up your bed and go home." And he rose and went home. *When the crowds saw it, they were afraid, and they glorified God, who had given such authority to men* (Mt 9:1–8).

The last phrase seems to refer to the power God gives to men to pardon sins. To be sure, here it refers to Jesus, but in the context of what St. Matthew tells us about the conferring of this power on the disciples (Mt 18:18) it seems clear that the Gospel narrative also contains a new perspective: the Church. The Church, too, does what formerly only Christ did; certain men have received from God the power to forgive sins. And today as well, men are amazed by that power.

One could develop this theme in relation to other matters, such as the liturgy and the Eucharist, but two points are now clear. First, in preserving the actions and words of Jesus, the apostles from the start emphasized their meaning. The Gospel accounts show little interest in the psychology of the actors: the concern is instead with the functional relationship to the mission of the Church. Second, although Jesus' words and actions were part of the oral teaching of the apostles, the similarities among the Gospels strongly suggest that in many cases they were put into writing to serve the needs of evangelization.

The Third Stage: The Writing of the Gospels

The third stage in the development of the Gospels is their writing as continuous narratives that are the work of individual authors. *Dei Verbum* describes the process like this:

> The sacred authors wrote the four Gospels, selecting some things from the many which had been handed on by word of mouth or in writing, reducing some of them to a synthesis, explaining some things in view of the situation of their churches and preserving the form of proclamation but always in such fashion that they told us the honest truth about Jesus. For their intention in writing was that either from their own memory and recollections, or from the witness of those who "themselves from the beginning were eyewitnesses and ministers of the Word" we might know "the truth" concerning those matters about which we have been instructed (cf. Lk 1:2–4).

This describes a true work of composition on the part of the Evangelists as actual authors (cf. *Dei Verbum*, no. 11) of what they wrote. In considering the nature of their work, it will be helpful to look at four elements: time of composition, place of composition, sources, and method of composition.

Generally speaking, the Gospels were composed between 60 and 90 A.D. The reason for this dating is obvious. The Fathers and ecclesiastical writers (Papias, St. Irenaeus, Clement of Alexandria, et al.) point out that the Gospels originated in the *need to preserve the preaching of the apostles*. For example:

> The Gospel according to St. Mark was begun in the following way. At the time that Peter was preaching the word in

Rome and explaining the Gospel under the action of the Spirit, those who were present in great number on that occasion *asked Mark, who since he had spent a great deal of time accompanying Peter and recalled the things that he had said, to put his words into writing.* This he did and he gave the Gospel to those who had asked for it. When he heard about this, Peter did not say anything either to prevent this nor to promote it. . . . But the last of all, John, knowing that the external things had already been clearly related in the Gospel, urged by his friends and inspired by the Holy Spirit, wrote a spiritual Gospel (Clement of Alexandria, according to Eusebius of Caesarea, *Ecclesiastical History*, 6,14,5–7).

Mark, having become the interpreter of Peter, wrote down accurately whatsoever he remembered. It was not, however, in exact order that he related the sayings or deeds of Christ. For he neither heard the Lord nor accompanied him. But afterwards, as I said, he accompanied Peter, who accommodated his instructions to the necessities [of his hearers], but with no intention of giving a regular narrative of the Lord's sayings. Wherefore Mark made no mistake in thus writing some things as he remembered them. For of one thing he took especial care, not to omit anything he had heard, and not to put anything fictitious into the statements. Matthew put together the oracles [of the Lord] in the Hebrew language, and each one interpreted them as best he could (Papias of Hierapolis, according to Eusebius of Caesarea, *Ecclesiastical History*, 3,39,14–15.16).

Matthew published among the Hebrews in their own language a written version of the Gospel, while Peter and Paul in Rome proclaimed the Gospel and founded the Church. It was after their death that Mark, *the disciple and interpreter of Peter, also transmitted in writing what had been preached by Peter. Luke, a companion of Paul, also put into a book what Paul had preached.* Later John, the disciple of our Lord, the same who had rested on his bosom, also wrote a Gospel while he was residing in Ephesus (St. Irenaeus, *Against Heresy*, 3,1,1).

The fourth of the Gospels [was] that of John, [one] of the disciples. When his fellow disciples and bishops urged him, he said: Fast with me from today for three days, and what will be revealed to each one let us relate to one another. In the same night it was revealed to Andrew, one of the apostles, that, whilst all were to go over [it], John in his own name should write everything down (*Muratorian Canon*).

The Gospels had their origin in the apostles—or their immediate disciples, although the authoritative sources are the apostles. They were written in the years when the apostles were dying out. The intention in the writing of the Gospels was to preserve the apostolic memory of Jesus Christ.

The place. In speaking of the Gospels' three stages we have seen that the setting for the first stage was Palestine and for the second the Roman Empire. The third stage involves particular persons—for example, Theophilus for Luke—or communities—Christians converts from Judaism along with Gentiles for Mark, Christians of Asia Minor for John.

At the same time, two things are common to them all. First, they are directed at Christians. These are no apologetical treatises for people who do not know Christianity. St. Luke writes to Theophilus "that you may know the truth of the things concerning which you have been informed" (Lk 1:4). The Gospel is not so much a new teaching as a verification or justification of teaching already received. Second, although each is directed to a well-defined group, all share the same universal destination: they are directed to the world. Even the most particular of the synoptics, St. Matthew, has this universal mission.

The source. *Dei Verbum* says the Evangelists worked with various sources. One source is what they "remembered." This appears to refer mainly to the Evangelists who were witnesses of the life of Jesus: according to tradition, Matthew and John. Elsewhere, *Dei Verbum* recalls that the apostles themselves were writers, and this could be applied also to the Evangelists. "Those apostles and other men associated with the apostles . . . under the inspiration of the same Holy Spirit, committed the message of salvation to writing" (*Dei Verbum*, no. 7). "The apostles preached, as Christ had charged them to do, and then, under the inspiration of the Holy Spirit, they and others of the apostolic age handed on to us in writing the same message they had preached" (*Dei Verbum*, no. 18).

A second source is the testimony of those who "took part from the beginning and were ministers of the word." Citing St. Luke, *Dei Verbum,* no.18 here refers to, if not two distinct sources, at least two distinct aspects of the sources: eyewitnesses and ministers of the word. It also speaks of written sources: i.e., the Evangelists took "data from the oral and written Tradition." In other words, part of the apostolic preaching was consigned to writing before the Gospels were composed.

This emphasizes the point already made: The ultimate source of the Gospels is the preaching of the apostles. Nor does *Dei Verbum* hesitate to repeat itself in affirming that the Evangelists worked under the inspiration of the Holy Spirit.

The work of composition. Finally, *Dei Verbum* speaks of what was personal in the work of each of the Evangelists.

> The sacred authors, in writing the four Gospels, selected certain of the many elements which had been handed on, either orally or already in written form, others they synthesized or explained with an eye to the situation of the Churches, the while sustaining the form of preaching, but always in such a fashion that they have told us the honest truth about Jesus. (*Dei Verbum*, no. 19)

This is to say that composing the Gospels involved editing: selecting, adapting, etc. Let us look at a simple example.

> Mt. 5:15: Nor do men light a lamp and put it under a bushel, but on a stand, and it gives light to all in the house.

> Lk 8:16: No one after lighting a lamp covers it with a vessel, or puts it under a bed, but puts it on a stand, that those who enter may see the light.

Matthew's text assumes a house in Palestine, where a lamp could light up a room and provide some light for adjoining rooms; Luke is thinking of a large house, Greek or Roman, in which a light does not illuminate the whole interior but helps those who enter to find their way. Examples to be considered in another chapter will show how such variations affected other, more important aspects: e.g., the contents of the Sermon on the Mount, concentrated in St. Matthew and diffused throughout the Gospel of St. Luke.

Another notable characteristic emphasized by *Dei Verbum* concerns style. The Gospels, it is said, retain the style of preaching. They do not aim to be a historical chronicle or apologetics or biography. Rather, they reproduce as faithfully as possible the apostolic preaching about Jesus Christ as the unique Savior of mankind.

4. CONCLUSION

Two important consequences for the reading and study of the Gospels follow from what has been said in this chapter.

First, it is very important not to confuse the three stages. The Gospels faithfully relate the actions of Jesus, but via the apostolic preaching and taking account of the audience.

Thus it is not necessary to affirm, for example, that the Sermon on the Mount, as it was written down by St. Matthew (Mt 5:2–7:29) in his Gospel, was preached by Jesus in exactly this way. Some authors think Matthew and Luke may be referring to two different addresses. Nevertheless, it seems easier to suppose that St. Matthew, on the occasion of the inaugural discourse of Jesus' ministry, gathers together the teachings of Jesus relating to the *renewal of the Law, but with a justice greater than that of the scribes and Pharisees* (Mt 5:20); while Luke (cf. Lk 6:17–49), for his part, offers a briefer compilation: 33 verses compared with the 111 verses of Matthew. This should not be taken as an eccentricity of St. Matthew. He expresses in this way the teaching of Christ himself and what was preached by the apostles.

One finds the same thing in other places. For example, chapter 10 of St. Matthew—like chapter 6 of St. Mark— provides a kind of rule for the apostolic mission. Much of the contents fit better with the mandate at the end of the Gospel or other episodes in Jesus' instruction of the twelve. Here they form a kind of protocol of the apostolic mission suited to that moment and to the whole life of the Church.

Second, in reading particular passages of the Gospels, it is necessary to keep in mind that before becoming part of the Gospel narrative, they were part of the Church's teaching, part of the liturgy, etc.—and part of the apostolic proclamation. To the extent that, with the help of the Holy Spirit, we strive to understand what the apostles and the ministers of the word wished to say, we can hear the very word of God preached by the apostles. For, like the whole of Sacred Scripture, the Gospels "are inspired by God and committed to writing once and for all time, they present God's own Word in an unalterable form, and they make the voice of the Holy Spirit sound again and again in the words of the prophets and apostles" (*Dei Verbum*, no. 21).

3

Methodologies

Juan Luis Caballero

As we have seen, no. 19 of *Dei Verbum* emphasizes the importance of both the preaching of the apostles and the work of those who put it in written form in composing the Gospels. God wanted to show us a truth, an aspect of Revelation, through these writings. But what truth? To know what God wanted to communicate, we must first determine *what the authors of the texts wanted to say (Dei Verbum,* no. 12). And to know that, one must study their work in its historical context: sources, editing, etc. This is the context for situating the various exegetical methodologies that have become systematized since the seventeenth century and especially in the nineteenth and twentieth centuries.

The eighteenth century witnessed the appearance of so-called critical exegesis. It is "critical" in respect to the tradition handed down and also from a methodological point of view, inasmuch as it applies to Scriptures the same instruments as are applied to other works of the past (although, paradoxically, without being critical of itself).

The first steps occurred in the study of the Old Testament, but the process later reached the New Testament as well. The studies have two principal aspects, diachronical and synchronical.

1. The diachronical centers on the history or formation of the text. Here are included textual criticism, historical

criticism and source criticism, form criticism, and redaction criticism.

Textual criticism directly confronts the problem of the original text. This type of investigation was carried on in the Renaissance era, in regard to the texts of classical works. Variations in the different manuscripts versions of the same text made it necessary to choose among the variants.

The seventeenth and eighteenth centuries brought diachronic approaches. First to appear were literary criticism or *source criticism* and *form criticism* dealing with stages prior to the final stage of a text, i.e., oral tradition and earlier writings.

Redaction criticism appeared in the twentieth century. It focused on the study of texts in their final form.

Historical criticism is not concerned with the history of a text's origins, but with the history behind the text. It seeks to shed light on the actions and events of which the text speaks.

2. Synchronic study addresses a text as a *consistent unity in a determined moment of time*, without reference to its historical evolution. Works of this kind study relations between constitutive elements of a text and its lines of significance. The most important forms of analysis used today are the narrative, the rhetorical, and the semiotic [symbolic].

    Finally, there is an approach that began especially after 1960 in literary studies and is also found in biblical studies: the history of a text's effects or *Rezeptionsgeschichte*. It investigates how interpretations given to a text at various times influence the present understanding of the text. It is assumed that "influence" does not signify a change in meaning, but a deepening and updating of meaning. Although the practical utility for biblical studies of this approach remains to be shown, it appears capable of supplying interesting insights by taking tradition into consideration in a scientific manner at the moment of reading, receiving, and transmitting a text.

1. Preparatory Stages of Analysis: Textual Criticism

To read a text it must first be established. We do not have the originals of ancient texts but copies, and the copies do not always coincide. The attempt to determine the original text is called *textual criticism.*

In the case of the New Testament, there is a multitude of handwritten texts and of citations in the works of the Fathers of the Church; these are in languages such as Greek, Latin, Syriac, and Coptic. Some 59 manuscripts contain the entire New Testament and some 2,000 only the Gospels. None of these is exactly the same as any other. The task of textual criticism is to determine which is the most trustworthy text while evaluating the different variants. It makes clear the care that has been taken in the transmission of something as central as the biblical text.

Most New Testament variants are insignificant for the meaning of the text. They are the result of errors by those making the copies, misunderstanding of the meaning of a text when copying it, a desire to correct, explain or comment, etc. Fenton Hort, a famous specialist of the nineteenth century, concluded that there is no textual problem with seven-eighths of the New Testament and only differences of minor importance with the rest. Of the 200,000 known variants, only 200 have any significance.

The second part of Lk 9:10 serves to illustrate what has been said. The English translation used in the Bible edited by the School of Theology of the University of Navarre says: "When the apostles returned, they told all that they had done; and, taking them with him, he retired apart to a city called Bethsaida." In other manuscripts or citations by the Fathers one can also find these readings: "to a village called Bethsaida"; "to a solitary place"; "to a village called Bethsaida, to a solitary place"; "to a solitary place of the city called Bethsaida"; "to a place called Bethsaida"; "to a place of the city called Bethsaida"; or the words are omitted entirely. Textual criticism tries to determine which is most likely the original text.

2. The Diachronic or (Pre)History of the Text

Once the text is established, analysis properly so-called can begin. There is a series of methodologies, including "diachronic" ones. The word diachronic, of Greek origin, means "across [or through or in the course of] time." Here, it refers to the origins or historical formation of texts.

This is easier to understand in the case of a written work. Normally a book is not written at a single sitting. First comes the selection of material, written or oral, one's own or borrowed; next the organization of the material according to the writer's plan; and finally the actual writing. Analyzing this process may point to questions about sources, literary forms, and editing.

This process is particularly interesting in the case of the synoptic Gospels, for here it is possible to compare three texts that speak about the same things but in different ways. Analysis of the "what" and "how" of each Evangelist can lead to a "why": i.e., *the idea or message that the final author of the text wanted to transmit and, therefore, his own conception or theological perspective about what he is writing.* This sheds light on a premise of the diachronical method: *to understand a text is equivalent to reconstructing its origin* and recognizing the distinct phases of its formation.

In what follows, various diachronic approaches are considered in the order in which, historically, they appeared (not the order in which they are applied to text). Note that the emergence of a new approach does not supercede earlier ones but normally integrates them or takes them for granted.

Source Criticism or "Literary" Criticism

The three synoptic Gospels: Matthew, Mark, and Luke, are called "synoptic" because likenesses and differences among them are immediately apparent. Sometimes they narrate different things, other times the same things but in a different way. St. John in some ways resembles the synoptics, but in general he relates things not related in the other three Gospels.

What were the sources of these several accounts? Was there a single source? These questions were considered in the early days of Christianity by authors like Origen in the third century (cf. his *Contra Celsum*) and St. Augustine at the beginning of the fifth century, with his *De Consensus Evangelistarum*. Source criticism returned to these questions many centuries later, but asked them in a new way, independently of the received tradition. These studies gave rise to the first ventures into the historical-critical sphere.

Source criticism undertakes to study the *written traditions* present in the prehistory of texts, reconstructing insofar as possible and investigating the circumstances in which they appeared. Specifically, it postulates that the Old Testament reflects a series of traditions and the settings in which they appeared and developed. For example, the traditions that gave rise to the Pentateuch were the priestly, the prophetic, etc. In regard to the New Testament, studies dealing with the sources of the synoptics are particularly numerous. Let us consider them.

In general, in dealing with the synoptic Gospels authors engaged in source criticism speak of:

1. Material common to all three, called the *triple tradition*: for example, the accounts of the Passion or the miracle of the calming of the storm. In general, they include almost the whole of the Gospel of St. Mark.

2. Material common to Matthew and Luke, but absent from Mark, the so-called *double tradition*, often referred to as "Q" (the letter stands for the German word *Quelle*—"source"); for example: the Sermon on the Mount.

3. Material *proper to each Evangelist*. Luke has the most (some fifty items, including the parables of the Good Samaritan and the Prodigal Son). Then comes Matthew (some thirty items, for example, the adoration of the Magi). Finally Mark (a very small number, for example, the cure of the deaf-mute in 7:32–37).

Differences also exist in the *sequence* and *formulation* of material. The sequence sometimes is the same in all three synoptics, but when it is not, Matthew and Luke never coincide with Mark; and Matthew and Luke tend to have a better style than Mark in passages common to all.

Over the centuries there have been various theories about the question of sources.

1. Summing up what was said by other Fathers of the Church, St. Augustine, in his *De Consensus Evangelistarum*, formulated a hypothesis regarding the *canonical order* of the books: Matthew was first, Mark composed a summary that took into account the preaching of Peter, and Luke wrote his Gospel for the pagans.

> These four Evangelists are very well known throughout the world. . . . This is the order in which they wrote, according to what is traditionally accepted: First Matthew, then Mark, in third place Luke, finally John. So the order in which they received and announced the Good News is one thing, and the order in which they

wrote it down is another. In knowledge and preaching, they were among the first followers of the Lord present in the flesh who, hearing him speak and seeing him act, were personally dispatched by him to evangelize. When it comes to the writing—and one must believe that this was done by God's command—two of those chosen by the Lord before his Passion, Matthew and John are respectively first and last. The other two were not part of the Twelve but they followed Christ, and he spoke through them, so they must be counted as his children (*De Consensus Evangelistarum*, 1, 1–2).

2. The first critical hypotheses, dating from the eighteenth century, fundamentally postulate two types of relationships among the Gospels: some speak of *interdependence* among them; others of *independent prior sources*.

One of the first and best-known exponents of interdependence was the German Johann Jakob Griesbach (1745–1812). He held that Matthew was the first to write; then Luke, knowing Matthew; and last of all, Mark who was acquainted with the other two. This basically coincides with the view of St. Augustine, though rearranging the order of the Gospels. F. Baur, founder of the liberal school of Tübingen, saw his theory about the early Church confirmed here. In his view, there was a Judaizing current, crystallized in the Gospel of St. Matthew, and a Hellenizing one, reflected in the Gospel of Luke; the Gospel of Mark was, as it were, a "catholic' synthesis.

An Oxford school, especially popular up to about 1970, is representative of the second tendency. It developed between the end of the nineteenth century and the first quarter of the twentieth. Burett Hillman Streeter, in *The Four Gospels: A Study of Origins* (1924), formulated its thinking as follows. The Gospels have four independent sources: "Q" (verses common to Matthew and Luke), "L" (the original source of Luke), "M" (a source peculiar to Matthew), and Mark (composed in Rome about the year 66). The combination of L and Q produced a Proto-Luke; and this, along with Mark and a document now included in Luke 1–2, produced the present Luke. Later, the combination of Q, M, and Mark produced the Gospel of Matthew. Followers of this theory now generally assume that a Q source and Mark existed originally. Note, however, that this is only a working hypothesis: *explanations* do not add up to *evidence*.

The tendency today is to keep literary questions separate as much as possible from matters of an ideological or historical nature. Since there is some basis for all the theories, all are kept in mind in the study of texts, and the one or ones that seem most applicable to a particular text are brought into play to explain it.

Form Criticism or *"Formgeschichte"*

Form criticism is the branch of historical-critical methodology with the greatest influence in the twentieth century, both in exegesis and in biblical commentary. It provides the background of *Dei Verbum*, no. 19. Among its major figures in regard to the Gospels have been Martin Dibelius, Karl Ludwig Schmidt, and Rudolph Bultmann. They published their first systematic treatments just after World War I—Dibelius and Schmidt in 1919, and Bultmann in 1921.

While accepting the criteria of source criticism, these authors postulated an *oral stage* preceding the written Gospels. This earlier stage consisted of *preaching the words and deeds of Jesus*, and took place in different contexts: the liturgy, preaching to the pagans, preaching to the Jews, apologetics, etc., with the largest part directed to Christians.

According to these authors, the preaching made use of popular writings associated with certain *particular occasions*; translated, developed, interpreted, and separated from their original context, these eventually formed part of the written Gospels. Thus the Gospels, in this view, were anthologies or collections of small literary units—sayings, parables, stories of cures, exorcisms, etc.—distinguishable from one another. The aim of the form critic was to reconstruct the original forms and contexts of those units.

Although Bultmann and Dibelius named and classified these forms in slightly different ways, they can in general be divided into "transmission of words" and "transmission of actions."

1. The *transmission of words* is of several kinds. There are *parables* (e.g., the lost sheep of Luke 15) and *sayings* (e.g., the instruction on reconciliation of Matthew 6:14–15: "For if you forgive men their trespasses, your heavenly Father also will forgive you; but if you do not forgive men their trespasses, neither will your Father forgive your trespasses." *Parenesis* or exhortations is another form (e.g., Mt 18:10: "See that you do not despise one of these little ones; for I tell you that in heaven their angels always behold the face of my Father who is in heaven").

   Bultmann classifies the sayings into: *sapiential* (Mk 3:24–26: "If a kingdom is divided against itself, that kingdom cannot stand. And if a house is divided against itself, that house will not be able to stand. And if Satan has risen up against himself and is divided, he cannot stand, but is coming to an end"); *prophetic* (Lk 7:22–23: "And he answered them, 'Go and tell John what you have seen and heard: the blind receive their sight, the lame walk, lepers are cleansed, and the deaf hear, the dead are raised up, the poor have good news preached to them. And blessed is he who takes no offense at me'"); and *legal* (Mt 5:31–32: "It was also said, 'Whoever divorces his wife, let him give her a certificate of divorce.' But I say to you that every one who divorces his wife, except on the ground of unchastity, makes her an adulteress; and whoever marries a divorced woman commits adultery"). There also are those which begin with "I tell you" and *comparisons* (Mk 8:35: "For whoever would save his life will lose it; and whoever loses his life for my sake and the gospel's will save it"). Generally speaking, the sayings are not long discourses.

2. With regard to the *transmission of actions*, the principal category is that of *paradigms* or *apothegms* combining sayings and deeds. (Dibelius spoke of "paradigms" and Bultmann of "apothegms"). These passages are brief and simple, with a conclusion that makes a point. For example: the account of the rich young man (Mk 10:17–31)—"How hard it will be for those who trust in riches to enter the kingdom of God!"; the episode of Martha and Mary (Lk 10:38–42)—"But only one thing is necessary"; the publicans and sinners—"I came not to call the righteous, but sinners" (Mt 9:13).

   There also are other, less important categories: for example, the accounts of *miracles*, where according to Dibelius the miracle is the teaching (as in the case of Jairus, Bartimeus, or the cure of the leper in Mark 1:40–45); *legends* (which show how God acts through the figure of Jesus, e.g., the twelve-year-old Jesus in the Temple); *myths* (a category of Dibelius's referring to depictions of Jesus as divine such as the Transfiguration); and other categories designated according to the prejudices of the one doing the designating.

Two central presuppositions relating to what is called *Sitz im Leben* [setting in life] are at work here. One is that these various forms, anonymously composed, were in circulation in the early community, so that the Evangelists were mere compilers. The other is that the primary purpose of these forms was not to preserve the memory of events in the life of the historical Jesus but only to provide material for preaching about him.

In its 1993 document *The Interpretation of the Bible in the Church*, the Pontifical Biblical Commission states that form history from the first gives rise to strong reservations since it studies texts through the lens of the history of religions. It is assumed that the early Church had no hesitation in mythologizing Jesus, and the texts were products of that process; the anonymous preachers functioned charismatically, composing forms as they needed them.

The ideas of form criticism lack objectivity even from a sociological point of view. The Church from the beginning was both *self-critical* and authoritative, accepting and rejecting material according to whether it was or was not in accord with what had actually taken place. Bultmann in particular places almost exclusive emphasis on the "functional" creativity of forms as determined by the circumstantial requirements (*Sitz im Leben*) of evangelization by the earliest Christian communities. However, both the origin and use of these accounts were *within* the Church—in the liturgy, for example.

Other, less serious objections can be raised to form criticism: for instance, the absence of agreement as to what the various forms are. If, moreover, everything was oral, why was it written down? As these examples suggest, one of the most important technical deficiencies of the method is lack of support in the texts.

While form criticism must still be taken into account, some of its conclusions are perhaps vitiated from the start. One illustration is the tendency of Protestant exegesis to find diverse churches in the New Testament—a finding probably attributable to the mindset of those who make it. At the same time, this kind of criticism—as we have said before—does call attention to some relevant aspects of the Gospels. Practiced with prudence, it is not only helpful but necessary for a better understanding of the sacred texts.

Redaction Criticism or *"Redaktionsgeschichte"*

By the middle of the twentieth century a historical method existed that had been enriched by the contributions of textual criticism, source criticism, and form criticism. Between 1950 and 1960, however, the process by which the Gospels were composed received a new scientific restatement.

Form criticism had emphasized an *oral tradition* of small literary units, *anonymous and popular*, while taking the Evangelists to be mere *compilers*. But professors such as Hans Conzelmann, Willi Marxsen, and Günther Bornkamm now sought to spotlight the particular emphases given by the *writers* of the Gospels to the traditions they used. These authors held that the emphases in question reflected the writers' situations and those of their readers.

Redaction criticism followed form criticism and complemented it. The emergence of form criticism coincided with an era of pessimism concerning the historical character of the Gospels; so, for instance, Bultmann's forms explained New Testament texts by the faith in Jesus of the communities in which the texts arose. Well purified, nevertheless, the method could be useful in describing the second stage in the composition of the Gospels, i.e., the stage of apostolic preaching. Redaction criticism coincided with a changed attitude toward the Gospels featuring greater trust in their historical value. From a methodological perspective, furthermore, it can be helpful in shedding light on the third stage present in the composition of the Gospels, namely, the work of the Evangelists.

Although this concern with "redaction" is already visible in St. Augustine, the first important systematic study of this kind appeared in 1948 when Bornkamm published an article showing the accounts of the storm on the lake in Matthew 8:23–27 and Mark 4:35–41 were a *teaching* about the disciples' lack of faith in the former, a *miracle* in the latter. The emphasis was changed in Matthew via slight modifications in the description of the event. Later more methodical studies included a 1952 article and 1954 book by Hans Conzelmann, published in English as *The Theology of Luke*, Willi Marxsen's *Mark the Evangelist: Studies on the Redaction History of the Gospel* (1956), and Wolfgang Trilling's *The Gospel according to St. Matthew* (1959).

To repeat, the aim of this analysis is to highlight and explain the *particular contribution* of each writer. This requires that we focus on the *general composition of the Gospels* and on their *stylistic elements*. In considering the first, we might reflect on how Matthew depicts Jesus as a teacher by placing the Sermon on the Mount after the selection of the first disciples, while in Mark, the role of the apostles is stressed. In Luke, the "road to Jerusalem" serves as an organizing principle. It is noteworthy, too, that each Gospel stresses particular themes: prayer in Luke, works in Matthew, etc.

Redaction criticism presupposes the results of source criticism and form criticism. The method has these phases: individual analysis of each passage; analysis of the connections among passages; and analysis of the composition of the text. This investigation can provide very interesting information: e.g., the theological perspective of each author, the historical context in which an author wrote. But it also has limits: excessive dependence on the theory of sources, a certain historical skepticism, exaggerations, subjectivism, etc. So, for instance, sometimes Conzelmann and Marxen, influenced by their own theological perspective, attribute so much importance to "their" Evangelists (Luke and Mark, respectively) that they treat them as very nearly the founders of Christianity.

3. SYNCHRONISM OR UNITY OF TEXT

Having examined the historical-critical methods, it remains to consider several complementary methods originating, in the latter years of the twentieth century, not in theology but the literary sciences. The generic name for them is synchronic methods. Historical-critical methodology is a kind of window opening on what lies behind texts. Synchronic methods focus, as it were, on the elements of the portrait: light, perspective, etc. This is to say, they study significant elements rather than contextual ones. Although many hands and many materials may have combined to produce the portrait, it is the portrait itself that matters. *Synchronic*, from the Greek, refers to what is *contemporaneous*; the implication is that, more than its history, the meaning of the text as it is is important.

Approaches of this kind which have produced the most interesting results in biblical exegesis in recent years are the narrative, the rhetorical, and the semiotic. No one model of biblical criticism takes in all the synchronic methods.

Narrative Analysis

Studies of narration are very ancient; a key work of this sort is the *Poetics* of Aristotle, written in the fourth century B.C. But it is precisely in the recent context that narrative theory has undergone a great development, influencing biblical studies in a decisive way. Given the narrative character of a large part of Sacred Scripture, this stands to reason.

Narration is *the description of an action*. But every action implies a *before* and an *after*. First there is an *initial situation*, then a particular *action* (words, deeds, etc.), then a *final situation*. Change, initiated by agents acting in particular circumstances, is central to narration. In the Gospel accounts, furthermore, what is important is not so much "what" happened as "how" and "why." The message of the narrative normally resides in the answers to those questions.

Take as a simple example the fourth chapter of the Gospel of St. John: the meeting between Jesus and the Samaritan woman at the well at Sichar. The woman went there simply for water, but after her conversation with Jesus she not only is on the way to conversion, but has become an apostle announcing someone who may be the Messiah to the people of her village; and in the end, having heard Jesus, they too believe. The change in the woman began in a personal encounter with Jesus that touched her conscience and led her to reflect on her past life, the need of water for a new life, and his position as Messiah: In revealing to the woman the truth about herself, Jesus also revealed himself to her and the reader.

No account can capture an event just as it happened. Accounts normally *select* some actions and persons and arrange them in a particular way. The narrator has a determining role, since the account is intimately linked to his or her way of understanding reality and the message he or she wants to transmit.

Let us consider three examples

In the parable of Lazarus and the rich man (Lk 16:19–31) we can distinguish two parts: the rich man and Lazarus while living, and the same two after death. Death is a turning point but also something more: what happens after their deaths illuminates their lives. The words of Abraham, speaking as it were for God, serve as our guide. The text shows that death not only brings a judgment, based on what one has done in life, but also seals human situations. The rich man admits he is guilty, yet he hopes to continue to use the poor man for his personal benefit. He also continues to call Abraham father, but although Abraham calls him his son, he has not received the inheritance—and so in life he cannot have been a true son of Abraham. The judgment passed on him reflects more than just his failure to care for Lazarus; the rich man and his brothers failed to heed God's revelation to all via Moses and the prophets and instead placed their trust in human goods. And since they refused to follow the ordinary path, they could not follow an extraordinary one—personal revelation from a dead man—that could only tell them what they ought already to have known.

cont'd.

> **examples** cont'd.
>
> The account of the possessed man of Gerasa (Mk 5:1–20) allows a similar analysis. The possessed man lived like an animal, but after his encounter with Jesus, he was converted into an apostle and preached to his family and friends. The account speaks not only of Jesus' power but of discipleship, in which not all should follow the same path. Two ideas are emphasized: Jesus cures so that those who are cured can become disciples; and Jesus wants to renew Israel from within Israel itself. The cured demoniac was a pagan and so was sent to preach to the pagans.
>
> Finally, an example that illustrates the narrative construction of the Gospels. The Gospel according to Mark clearly delineates the figure of Peter and his transformation, from one who gives himself in a spontaneous and unreflecting manner, to someone conscious of his weakness. Jesus' treatment of Peter drives this process of change; and even after Peter's disloyalty, Jesus mercifully welcomes him back. After his three denials, Peter becomes the foundation, the rock, whom Jesus seeks. He knows his own weakness, but he acts now with the strength of Jesus.

These examples, admittedly not analyzed deeply here, suggest how narrative analysis can help us to be good readers, noting the significant points in a text, contrasts, changes of direction, etc.

Rhetorical Analysis

Rhetoric was among the most prestigious disciplines of classical times. Prestigious figures like Quintilian, Cicero, Anaximenes, and Aristotle undertook to treat it systematically. Only recently, however, has rhetorical analysis been brought to bear upon biblical exegesis.

In general terms, rhetoric is concerned with oral discourse and, in Bible studies, with religious or sacred discourse. Rhetorical analysis seeks to understand how the Bible speaks and what it means to say. It does not study the sources of a text but its message, both the intention of the author or editor and the effect of the text on today's readers.

In classical rhetoric, intention and effect normally were functions of persuasive arguments. However, the authors of the New Testament were not seeking to persuade but to communicate; for this reason, it is better in this case to speak of efficacious discourse. The authors of the New Testament make use of sacred language, whose basic characteristic is authoritative proclamation, not rational persuasion. Although they employ literary resources—order and sequences in what is recounted, both in sections of the work or the work as a whole, propositions sustained in discourses and proofs, paradoxes, irony, etc.—their fundamental resources nevertheless are the origin and authority of the message, the perceived qualities in the speaker, etc. Also in the specific case of the Bible, appeal often is made to reason as the ground for accepting what is proclaimed: for example, by the citing of historical evidence.

The authors of the Gospels obviously belong to their cultural environment. Thus it is important to understand the rhetorical conventions of that era, both Semitic and classical.

Three categories come into play: judicial, deliberative, and persuasive. *Invention*, *disposition*, and *style* are operative in each.

Here is an example of the application of rhetorical analysis to the Gospels. Just before the Sermon on the Mount, Jesus is shown passing through the crowd and curing the sick. Although the sermon does not refer to this activity, it constitutes a background that enhances his authority when he speaks. After the sermon, he performs another miracle and so confirms his power. This miracle is a "sign" that has the character of evidence among the Jews. It is an irrefutable proof. The discourse proper runs from Matthew 5:2 to Matthew 7:28. Jesus does not refer to external proofs—miracles, prophecies fulfilled, etc.; all this came at an earlier stage of his mission. This second stage is the preaching of a message. Those around him are his disciples, witnesses who are themselves an external proof. When Jesus speaks, he anticipates a possible objection: "Don't think that I have come to abolish the Law and the Prophets; I have come not to abolish them but to fulfill them" (Mt 5:17).

A detailed study would bring many more details to light. Here Jesus gives a series of counsels on the conduct of life. All are oriented toward a new life, of which the beatitudes, found at the beginning of the discourse, are a foundation and a precondition. Matthew expresses all this by means of the rhetorical technique of a framework constructed for his readers' benefit.

Like any other synchronic analysis, rhetorical analysis has advantages and limitations. In some cases it is only descriptive, so that its interest is merely stylistic. In other cases, because the rhetoric of the New Testament is not shaped according to a priori rules, there is a risk of changing the text's meaning by forcing it to fit some inapplicable preconception.

Semiotic Analysis

Semiotic analysis was largely developed in the twentieth century. While the structuralism of the Swiss linguist Ferdinand de Saussure (1857–1913) is operative in its origins, its contemporary application to biblical studies above all reflects the work of Algirdas Julien Greimas (1917–1992), a French linguist of Lithuanian origin.

In general terms, semiotics is the *study of the production of significance.* The unit of study is the sign, not only as a verbal expression, but also in reference to reality. *Any reality is susceptible to being tuned into a sign, even the sign of a different reality.* For example, a snail, besides being a tiny animal, can also be a sign for exasperating slowness.

Semiotic analysis examines how a meaning is produced through *contrasts*. The contrast can be that involved in a relationship, normally that of opposed things or contraries. Analysis of these oppositions gives rise to the semiotic framework, which guides the interpretation of the meaning. Examples will help clarify this.

Having made a semiotic inventory of the account of the rich young man (Mk 10:17–31), we can establish a series of oppositions, as follows.		
Rich/riches/attachment to family	is opposed to	Poverty/leaving all
The first	is opposed to	The divine/kingdom of God
Affliction, going away sad	is opposed to	Treasure in heaven/brethren
Much at last	is opposed to	Much at first
From these data we can construct a semiotic framework reflecting the contraries and contradictions that comprise the significance of the text.		
Riches		Treasure in heaven
Attachment to family and riches		Adhesion to Jesus, Following
There is no treasure in heaven		There are no riches
There is no adhesion to Jesus		Detachment from family and riches

As this suggests, the meaning of the account in Mark could be stated this way. Riches in this world are contrary to treasure in heaven. Riches and attachment to family are contrary to the absence of riches and detachment from family; while the following of Jesus and treasure in heaven are contrary to lack of adhesion to Jesus and lack of treasure in heaven. Lack of riches and detachment from family are presuppositions for adhering to and following Jesus and having treasure in heaven; while not following Jesus and absence of treasure in heaven are related to attachment to riches and to family, which is contrary to what Jesus asked of the rich young man.

Our second example is the story of the prodigal son (Lk 15:11–32). The lines of meaning are concentrated in a marked opposition of "life" to "death," exemplified in "loss/ reencounter" and "sin/conversion." "Life" is represented here by life in the bosom of one's family, being welcomed upon returning, restoration of the signs of dignity, and by the festive celebration; and by the "non-death" of entering into oneself, voluntary humiliation, recognizing one's guilt and asking forgiveness. This is opposed to "death," as represented by separation, leaving what is common, egoistic extravagance, self-recovery based on scorn for the "non-life" of bare survival and loss of personal identity and even human dignity. Besides these oppositions stand certain relations: loss of what one had (squandering), which results in loss of being (degradation); as opposed to the gain of being (forgiveness granted, renewed dignity), which results in gaining possessions (reintegration into the family community).

Semiotics starts with a very helpful idea for scriptural exegesis: taking the texts as a *consistent whole*. The principal drawback is the *lack of reference to realities exterior to the text*, which diminishes the Bible's meaning. The Gospels speak of real events that happened in history, and they are directed to readers of all times. Concentrating exclusively on formal aspects will produce results that fall short of the requirements of biblical exegesis.

4

The Gospel According to St. Matthew

Vicente Balaguer

Now we turn to the works of the Evangelists. As in the other chapters, the objective is not to examine the Gospels closely, but simply to supply information that will help one read them better.

First we should cover author and date and place of composition, citing the information found in simple manuals and the introductions in many Bibles, followed by some questions that are the object of scientific discussion or involves slight differences of opinions.

This will be followed by a treatment of the literary and theological characteristics of the Gospel in question. The literary and the theological are joined here because the focus is not so much on technical characteristics—is the Gospel in good or bad Greek?—as on the way literary characteristics are related to the message. Here is an approach to understanding Jesus and the Gospel.

Next we shall consider the structure of the Gospel, with the aim of situating individual passages in relation to the whole. Limitations of space make it impossible to cover every passage, but the general sketch of each Gospel provides a framework for reading it.

Last come the principal contents of the Gospel and above all what it teaches about Jesus. Each Evangelist stresses certain themes, and keeping these in mind is a help to understanding the message.

1. AUTHOR, PLACE, AND DATE OF COMPOSITION

The text of the first Gospel, like the other three, does not contain the author's name. But, in the manuscripts—papyri and codices—it, like the others, is always preceded by an inscription: "Gospel according to Matthew." This indicates two things.

First, the text is linked to its origin and thereby to the authority of its author, i.e., an apostolic authority. This authority is special. The Gospels proceed from the apostles or from their disciples.

Second, the expression "according to Matthew," "according to Mark," etc. contrast with the titles given works of that era, which used the genitive of origin, "of." The significance seems to reside in an idea often repeated in early Christianity, namely, that there is only one Gospel, the Gospel of Jesus Christ (Mk 1:1). To say "according to St. Matthew" implies that what follows is the witness or testimony of St. Matthew.

The Author

Ancient written testimonies assure us that St. Matthew was the first to put the Gospel of Jesus Christ into writing. Papias, second-century bishop of Hierapolis, says that "Matthew prepared the discourses [about] of the Lord in the language of the Jews, and each one interpreted them as he could" (cf. Eusebius of Caesarea, *Ecclesiastical History*, 3,39,16).

No copy of this text of Matthew mentioned by Papias has been preserved, nor has any description of it, so it is not known whether Papias meant a Hebrew or an Aramaic text. Nor is it known whether the discourses in question were the whole Gospel or only the words of our Lord. On the other hand, the Greek Gospel of Matthew was used as an authoritative and canonical text from very early on.

All of the ancient documents attribute this first Gospel to Matthew, the tax collector. There is a certain confirmation in the text of the Gospel itself, since it is the only one in which the name Matthew is used to designate the publican whom our Lord called at the beginning of his public life (Mt 9:9–12) and who coincides with "Matthew, the publican" (Mt 10:3) named in the lists of the twelve (Mt 10:1–14; cf. Mk 3:13–10; Lk 6:12–16; Acts 1:13). St. Luke says he was called Levi, while in St. Mark, Levi the son of Alpheus (Lk 5:27; Mk 2:14).

The Audience

Many features in the Gospel of St. Matthew suggest that the intended audience was Jews who had embraced the Christian faith. For example, there are many expressions of Palestinian origin used only by this Gospel: "kingdom of heaven" (Mt 3:2; 4:17, etc.), "Heavenly Father" (Mt 5:48; 6:14, 26; etc.), "the holy city" (Mt 4:5; 27:53), "House of Israel" (Mt 15:24), "the flesh and the blood" (Mt 16:17), "to bind and to loose" (Mt 16:19; 18:18), etc. Much more than the other Evangelists, too, the author refers to Jewish customs: the offering on the altar, the conduct of the priests on the Sabbath, the use of phylacteries, etc. (Mt 5:23; 12:5; 23:5).

Furthermore, the text is permeated with explicit citations from the Old Testament illustrating Jesus' fulfillment of the promises of God to the people of Israel (as many as 150 references, with 50—compared with 23 in each of the other two synoptics—containing explicit citations). The author also uses methods of interpreting Sacred Scripture proper to the scribes of Israel: the *gematria*—use of numbers to signify things—in the genealogy, the use of the divine passive to avoid pronouncing the name of God, etc.

Finally, Matthew more than anyone collects the words of our Lord explaining relations between the Old and the New Law. For instance: "Think not that I have come to abolish the Law and the Prophets; I have come not to abolish them but to fulfill them. For truly I say to you, till heaven and earth pass away, not an iota, not a dot, will pass from the law until all is accomplished" (Mt 5:17–18).

The Place of Composition

While the Gospels have a universal outlook, it has always been thought that the first Gospel was written in Antioch of Syria, a city well known from the Acts of the Apostles and famous for its evangelizing vigor. Supporting this hypothesis is the fact that both the *Didache* and the letters of St. Ignatius of Antioch—documents from the end of the first century that originated in Antioch—cite sayings of our Lord using the same formulas found in Matthew.

The Date of Composition: Other Circumstances

Closer examination of the text of the Gospel and the historical circumstances of the origin shed additional light on these matters.

So, with regard to audience, the Acts of the Apostles shows that the Church of Antioch was not composed only of Jews who had embraced the new faith but also of Gentile converts to Christianity. Matthew's Gospel does not suppose only a mission to Jews but universal outreach: for example, in calling Christians "the salt of the earth" and "the light of the world" (cf. Mt 5:13–14), or reporting the final command to make disciples "of all nations" (Mt 28:19). It is reasonable to suppose that the community Matthew was addressing was made up of Jews and Gentiles. To both he taught the value of the Law in relation to Christ: the Gentiles so that they would respect it, the Jews so that they would fulfill it in the way suited to new life in Jesus Christ.

With regard to date of composition, even though Matthew used expressions of Palestinian origin and reference to Jewish customs of our Lord's day, and Papias said Matthew wrote in the language of the Hebrews, nevertheless the Greek of Matthew's Gospel is good; it avoids vulgarisms and uses proper expressions. It does not resemble a word-for-word translation of a Hebrew text. As for Papias's claim ("Matthew arranged the discourses about the Lord in the language of the Hebrews, and each interpreted them as they could"), it is arguable. Matthew, as we shall see, is remarkably clear in setting forth doctrine, which does not square with "each interpreted them as he could." In addition, St. Matthew seems to be acquainted with the Gospel of Mark, and where a passage of the latter is obscure, he explains it with more precision.

Thus, scholars suppose Papias is speaking of a text in Aramaic written very early, around 50 or 60 A.D., and later used by St. Luke, as well as the writer of the canonical Gospel of St. Matthew, who reproduced it in substance but wrote directly in Greek. This Gospel of St. Matthew in Greek, inspired and canonical, may have been written between the years 80 and 90. This dating reflects the fact that the text seems to have been written as a polemic against the interpretation of the Law made by Jews who had not embraced Christianity following the Romans' destruction of the Temple in the year 70.

2. Literary and Theological Characteristics

All of the Gospels are directed to believers. All try to teach who Jesus is and the importance of his teachings, but each in its own way. Bearing this in mind helps one derive more from reading them. Perhaps the most significant feature of Matthew is its catechetical emphasis. His Gospel is in many respects like a catechism—a teaching text that answers questions a Christian might have. As Pope John Paul II pointed out, St. Matthew's account has been called "the Gospel of the catechist" and St. Mark's "the Gospel of the catechumen" (John Paul II, *Catechesis Tradendae*, no. 11).

"Gospel of the catechumen" signifies that Mark's text led people to embrace the Christian faith. "Gospel of the catechist" means that Matthew's account explains that faith. It is often said that the author applied our Lord's counsel in Matthew 13:52 to himself: "Every scribe who has been trained for the kingdom of heaven is like a householder who brings out of his treasure what is new and what is old." He proposes the teaching of Christ as the basis of a way of life.

At the end of the Gospel, our Lord says:

> All authority in heaven and on earth has been given to me. Go therefore and make disciples of all nations, baptizing them in the name of the Father and of the Son and of the Holy Spirit, *teaching them to observe all that I have commanded you*; and lo, I am with you always, to the close of the age. (Mt 28:19–20)

The phrase in italics makes it clear that the apostles are to teach and guard the norms commanded by the Lord. And that is what St. Matthew does. For example, the Our Father as presented by Matthew in the Sermon on the Mount has four principal elements.

1. "And when you pray, you must not be like the hypocrites; for they love to stand and pray in the synagogues and at the street corners, that they may be seen by men. Truly, I say to you, they have received their reward. But when you pray, go into your room and shut the door and pray to your Father who is in secret; and your Father who sees in secret will reward you."

2. "And in praying do not heap up empty phrases as the Gentiles do; for they think that they will be heard for their many words. Do not be like them, for your Father knows what you need before you ask him."

3. "Pray then like this: Our Father who art in heaven, hallowed be thy name. Thy kingdom come. Thy will be done, on earth as it is in heaven. Give us this day our daily bread; and forgive us our debts, as we also have

;iven our debtors; and lead us not into temptation, but deliver us from evil."

4. "For if you forgive men their trespasses, your heavenly Father also will forgive you; but if you do not forgive men their trespasses, neither will your Father forgive your trespasses." (Mt 6:5–15)

What is the prayer of the Christian like? (1) It is not ostentatious like that of the Pharisees, (2) nor is it full of words like that of the Gentiles. (3) It is filial, simple, and sincere like the Lord's prayer. And (4) should be accompanied by works which show its authenticity.

Obviously, each aspect of this teaching can be enriched by other Gospel passages. For example, forgiveness of offenses is illustrated by the parable of the servant whose debt of ten thousand talents is forgiven but who cannot forgive a small debt owed to him (Mt 18:22–29), etc. But although Matthew did not say everything about prayer here, he said a lot. These words of the first Gospel provide an ideal starting point for anyone who wants to know how to pray or wants to teach others.

This catechetical aspect of St. Matthew also is apparent in chapter 18, the "discourse on the Church," which contains norms to govern ecclesial life. For example:

1. How to act in relation to those who are weaker or less instructed? The answer is supplied in the maxims against scandal (Mt 18:1–11).

2. How to behave with one's brother who weakens and might perish? The parable of the lost sheep (Mt 18:12–14).

3. How to deal with a backslider? The teaching on fraternal correction (Mt 18:15–17).

4. How far must one go in forgiving? Consider how much God has forgiven us (Mt 18:21–35).

Here, too, we find our Lord's statement concerning the power of the Church's ministers. "Truly, I say to you, whatever you bind on earth shall be bound in heaven, and whatever you loose on earth shall be loosed in heaven" (Mt 18:18).

This is very similar to what Jesus tells Peter after his confession at Caesarea Philippi. "Whatever you bind on earth shall be bound in heaven, and whatever you loose on earth shall be loosed in heaven" (Mt 16:19).

Evidently the phrase describes the power our Lord has given his ministers in the Church. There is a commentary on this in the account of how Jesus forgave the sins of the paralytic at Capernaum, and cured him. At the end one finds this comment: "When the crowds saw it, they were afraid, and they glorified God, who had given such authority to men" (Mt 9:8). God can give man power to forgive sins. Jesus had it, and he gave it to his ministers in the Church.

St. Matthew has other ways of teaching. For example, scholars have noted that the rhythmic quality of our Lord's words in this Gospel facilitates remembering and repeating them.

Next we shall consider two other dimensions of the Gospel's catechetical character: the long discourses and the manner of narrating the miracles.

The Discourses

Matthew has sometimes been called *the Gospel of our Lord's discourses*. Among these are invectives against and controversies with the Pharisees and scribes (Mt 23:13–36; 12:25–45). But five, which close with words like ". . . and when Jesus finished these sayings" (Mt 7:28; 11:1; 13:53; 19:1; 26:1), are teaching discourses.

Mt 5:1–7:29: *The Sermon on the Mount*. St. Augustine called this *perfectae vitae christianae modus*—"the perfect way of Christian life." It describes precisely how the Christian should act, according to a justice superior to that of the scribes and Pharisees.

Mt 10:1–42: *The missionary discourse to the apostles.* This discourse is relevant not only to the mission of the twelve to Israel but also refers to the apostolic mission of the Church. It is a sketch of how to proclaim Christ's message.

Mt 13:1–2: *The discourse of the parables.* These parables speak about the Kingdom of God and indicate the appropriate response to various situations in the life of the Church. As the parable of the sower points out, not everyone who accepts the message will persevere to the end, but those who do will reap a great reward. We are told not to be discouraged because the kingdom, the Church, grows slowly, like the mustard seed; not to be concerned because the good fruit of the message grows alongside the bad sown by the devil in the form of "tares" or noxious weeds; and not to be anxious, since in the end God will judge, etc.

Mt 18:1–35: *The ecclesiastical discourse.* This was discussed earlier. It contains teaching about the behavior of the faithful in the Church.

Mt 24:1–25, 46: *The eschatological dialogue.* This consoling discourse speaks of difficulties that will arise in the development of the Church over the centuries: external difficulties resulting from persecution, internal difficulties resulting from the cooling of love, etc. The Christian's foundation is hope; neither now nor at the end of time will Christ abandon his own.

The Miracles

By contrast with the liveliness of St. Mark, the accounts of miracles in St. Matthew are much more stylized and solemn, with fewer picturesque details. But this serves to underline the mission of Jesus (the Christological aspect), the faith of those who come to Jesus (there is a close relationship between what is asked and what is granted), and the place of the disciples, who represent the Church. From this perspective, the Gospel is an example of Christian catechesis. A few texts will help to illustrate this.

Mt 15:21–28	Mk 7:24–30
And Jesus went away from there and withdrew to the district of Tyre and Sidon. And behold, a Canaanite woman from that region came out and cried, "Have mercy on me, O Lord, Son of David; my daughter is severely possessed by a demon." But he did not answer her a word. And his disciples came and begged him, saying, "Send her away, for she is crying after us." He answered, "*I was sent only to the lost sheep of the house of Israel.*" But she came and knelt before him, saying, "Lord, help me." And he answered, "It is not fair to take the children's bread and throw it to the dogs." She said, "Yes, Lord, yet even the dogs eat the crumbs that fall from their masters' table." Then Jesus answered her, "*O woman, great is your faith! Be it done for you as you desire.*" And her daughter was healed instantly.	And from there he arose and went away to the region of Tyre and Sidon. And he entered a house, and would not have any one know it; yet he could not be hid. But immediately a woman, whose little daughter was possessed by an unclean spirit, heard of him, and came and fell down at his feet. Now the woman was a Greek, a Syro-phoenician by birth. And she begged him to cast the demon out of her daughter. And he said to her, "Let the children first be fed, for it is not right to take the children's bread and throw it to the dogs." But she answered him, "Yes, Lord; yet even the dogs under the table eat the children's crumbs." And he said to her, "For this saying you may go your way; the demon has left your daughter." And she went home, and found the child lying in bed, and the demon gone.

St. Mark adopts the point of view of the woman who seeks Jesus, makes her appeal to him with insistence and daring, and returns home having obtained what she sought. St. Matthew's special emphasis is visible in the two italicized passages. In the first, Jesus' words underline his mission as Messiah and supply a reason for his resistance to performing the cure required of him. As for the second, similar words appear elsewhere in the Gospel (Mt 8:13, to the centurion:

"Go and be it done as you have believed"; Mt 8:29, to the blind men: "May it be done to you according to your faith"). The emphasis is on faith: those who have faith receive what they ask for.

Let us look at another example: the cure of Peter's mother-in-law.

Mt 8:14–15	Mk 1:29–31
"And when Jesus entered Peter's house, he saw his mother-in-law lying sick with a fever; he touched her hand, and the fever left her, and she rose and served him.	And immediately he left the synagogue, and entered the house of Simon and Andrew, with James and John. Now Simon's mother-in-law lay sick with a fever, and immediately they told him of her. And he came and took her by the hand and lifted her up, and the fever left her; and she served them.

St. Mark's narrative is typical of his lively style. We are told that the disciples accompanied Jesus, that they spoke to him about the person in need, that after the cure they were served along with him. In St. Matthew the focus is on catechesis. The anecdotal details are missing, the disciples disappear, except for Simon—who is given his name in the Church, Peter. Jesus cures the woman without any request; and once she has been cured, the woman, like a disciple in the Church, serves him.

3. STRUCTURE OF THE GOSPEL

In considering the structure of the Gospel, we seek to understand each passage in context: the immediate context, the context of the whole Gospel, or the context of the ministry of Jesus. Normally, the Evangelist's aim can be discerned from certain indications accessible to an attentive reading. In the case of St. Matthew, two significant features will serve as a starting point.

1. As many as ninety times, incidents and episodes are introduced by "then." But only three times—at the beginning of Jesus' public ministry, after the confession of Peter, and at the betrayal of Judas—is the expression "From that time . . ." used.

    Mt 4:17: "From that time Jesus began to preach, saying, 'Repent, for the kingdom of heaven is at hand.'"

    Mt 16:21: "From that time Jesus began to show his disciples that he must go to Jerusalem and suffer many things from the elders and chief priests and scribes, and be killed, and on the third day be raised."

    Mt 26:15–16: "*And they paid him thirty pieces of silver.* And from that moment he sought an opportunity to betray him."

    These three passages clearly mark out three periods in the activity of Jesus: the period in—especially—Galilee, where he proclaimed the kingdom with deeds and words before the people; the period after the confession of Peter at Caesarea Philippi, where Jesus' teaching regarding the disciples' salvific mission is very important; and the period in which the drama of his death and glorious resurrection unfolded. This threefold division suggests a possible structure.

2. On the other hand, as has been said, the first Gospel conveys the impression of a carefully planned structure which itself has a catechetical purpose. Five discourses of our Lord are followed by five narrative sections referring to messianic signs performed by Jesus. Some authors see here an allusion to the five books of the Law, the Pentateuch, which also speak of the special actions of God with his people and contain his commandments. The idea of a

parallel may seem a bit strained, but it is clear enough that we are not meant to see what Jesus does merely as the fulfillment of God's promises; rather they should also be seen as inaugurating a new people, the Church, which was born of Jesus.

4. Principal Contents

It is clear that the primary teaching of all of the Gospels turns on Jesus Christ and on his work. Who he is and his importance for mankind's salvation are revealed by his actions and words and by those who approach him. If one were to organize the teachings of the first Gospel in categories, I believe this could be done by the use of two ideas: the person of Jesus Christ and the Church he founded. The two things are related.

Jesus Christ

Jesus, as St. Mark depicts him, is notable especially for his majesty—a majesty visible now in a Byzantine mosaic or the image of Christ the Pantocrator in a medieval church: true man and, at the same time, true God and Lord of all creation. In St. Matthew, these characteristics are best expressed by the titles applied to Jesus.

The Son of God. First among these is *the Son of God*. From Jesus' conception by the action of the Holy Spirit to the Trinitarian formula for Baptism at the end, St. Matthew affirms and insists that Jesus is the Son of God (Mt 1:30; 28:19). The voice from heaven declares this at the Baptism and at the Transfiguration. So does Jesus himself.

> I thank thee, Father, Lord of heaven and earth, that thou hast hidden these things from the wise and understanding and revealed them to babes; yea, Father, for such was thy

gracious will. All things have been delivered to me by my Father; and no one knows the Son except the Father, and no one knows the Father except the Son and any one to whom the Son chooses to reveal him. (Mt 11:25–27)

St. Matthew invests this idea of Jesus as Son of God with several layers of meaning.

1. Recounting the return of Joseph to Nazareth, he says: "[He] remained there until the death of Herod. This was to fulfill what the Lord had spoken by the prophet, 'Out of Egypt have I called my son' " (Mt 2:15).

    The son to whom the prophet Hosea refers is Israel. But Israel, as a son of God, did not fulfill the God-given mission to make all nations holy. Jesus, the Son of God, carried out this mission that Israel did not know how to fulfill. But it is important to note Matthew's reasoning: Jesus is not the Son of God because of the number of allusions to him in the Old Testament; rather, as the Son of God that he was, he fulfilled the promises God entrusted to his chosen ones, Israel.

2. Jesus' divinity also is affirmed by the title *Emmanuel, God with us*. The Child had this title from his conception (Mt 1:23); Jesus uses a paraphrase to affirm his presence in the midst of the Church: "For where two or three are gathered in my name, there am I in the midst of them" (Mt 18:20).

    This is more meaningful in the light of a saying in the times of our Lord: "If two sit together and the words between them are not those of the Torah, then it is a session of mockers . . . but if two sit together and the words between them are those of the Torah, then the *Shejina* [the divine presence] is in the midst of them" (Rabbi Hananiah ben Teradyon, in the *Mishnah*, Abot 3,2).

    Jesus' words clearly allude to his being consubstantial with the Father; and the same is true of a third text, at the end of the Gospel, where, when sending forth his disciples, our Lord uses a gloss on the name Emmanuel to affirm his presence in the midst of the Church until the end of times: "And lo, I am with you always, to the close of the age" (Mt 28:20).

As God was with Israel in the desert and with the guides of his people (Moses, Joshua, etc.), so Jesus will be with the Church until the end of the world. One could not more eloquently say that Jesus is God and the Church the People of God.

Son of Man and Servant of the Lord. It is in the light of this essential name, the Son of God, that all the other messianic titles by which the Old Testament pre-announced the Savior acquire their most profound meaning. These other titles are Son of David, King, Son of Man, Messiah.

Jesus is the *Son of Man*. Jesus uses this name for himself throughout the Gospel, and it is not without ambiguity. Son of Man is, on the one hand, the equivalent of man. On the other hand, in the tradition of Israel, inaugurated in the image of Daniel 7:13–14, it designates the transcendent personage to whom God gives "dominion and glory and kingdom, that all peoples, nations, and languages should serve him," and whose "dominion is an everlasting dominion, which shall not pass away." Thus, the title designates a true man, but one who is transcendent. St. Matthew, starting with his genealogy, points out how it is possible that Jesus be a true man of the line of David and also of divine origin.

But the task of Jesus, true man, is delineated above all in the fulfillment of his mission as the humble *Servant of the Lord*, prophesied by Isaiah, who with his words and miracles fulfills God's salvific plan for mankind. In St. Matthew's version of events, Jesus' primary reason for performing miracles is not compassion for the multitude, the alleviation of suffering, and so on; it is to fulfill God's plan, as it is sketched out in the second part of the prophet Isaiah. Two texts will serve to illustrate this point.

> That evening they brought to him many who were possessed with demons; and he cast out the spirits with a word, and healed all who were sick. This was to fulfill what was spoken by the prophet Isaiah, "He took our infirmities and bore our diseases." (Mt 8:16–17)

> Jesus, aware of this, withdrew from there. And many followed him, and he healed them all, and ordered them not to make him known. This was to fulfill what was spoken by the prophet Isaiah: "Behold, my servant whom I have chosen, my beloved with whom my soul is well pleased. I will put my Spirit upon him, and he shall proclaim justice to the Gentiles. He will not wrangle or cry aloud, nor will any one hear his voice in the streets; he will not break a bruised reed or quench a smoldering wick, till he brings justice to victory; and in his name will the Gentiles hope." (Mt 12:15–21)

But the Servant of the Lord is not only God's chosen one; he also suffered rejection by his fellow Jews. St. Matthew includes teachings and events that illuminate the mystery of the *rejection of Jesus, the promised Messiah*, on the part of the Jewish leaders, who carried along with them a good part of the people. The Evangelist responds to that mystery in various ways: sometimes by relating stages in Jesus' rejection by scribes, Pharisees, and leaders of the priests; other times by narrating his sufferings during his Passion, thereby making it clear that those events did not frustrate the Divine plan but were foreseen and announced by the Prophets, and are its fulfillment (Mt 12:17; 13:35; 26:54, 56; 27:9; etc.). For that reason our Lord says God's promise will be given to another people who will make a return of its fruits (Mt 21:43). That new people is the Church.

The Church

St. Matthew's Gospel has been called the "ecclesiastical" Gospel, for several reasons. Not only does the name *Church* appear there three times (Mt 16:18; and 18:17 [twice]) but, without being expressly named, the Church can be glimpsed in the background of the narrative. Here we have especially underlined this aspect. We have seen how a Christian who reads the Gospel can find answers to questions that arise as part of everyday life in the Church: how to pray, how to fast, how to behave with one's brethren, how to carry out the apostolic mission, the extent of one's duty to obey the commandments of the Law, etc. And there are answers to other questions as well: why one should forgive sins on earth, why many Jews, to whom the message of Christ was primarily directed, did not respond to God's invitation in Jesus Christ, why Peter has a principal role in the Church, etc.

There are many more such examples in St. Matthew—so much so that a well-known researcher called his commentary on Matthew: "The True Israel." This theme informs the Gospel from start to finish. If, as the opening genealogy shows, the people of Israel are the descendants of Jacob, the first Israel, the Church is comprised of the descendants of Jesus, and is established by his work. And at the end, the missionary mandate includes, as was the practice in Israel, the making of disciples. Jesus' command to make disciples of all peoples signals the fulfillment of God's destiny for Israel: to be the instrument of salvation for the whole world. That destiny is fulfilled by the Church, "the true Israel."

5

The Gospel According to St. Mark

Vicente Balaguer

1. AUTHOR, PLACE, AND DATE OF COMPOSITION

Authorship and place and date of composition are inter-related in the case of the Gospel of Mark. St. Mark, not one of the apostles but a disciple of the apostles, wrote at the request of the Church at the time of Peter's death, to preserve the preaching of that apostle.

The Author

Tradition is unanimous in affirming that the author of the second Gospel is Mark, "the disciple and interpreter" of Peter. (In Eusebius of Caesarea's *Historia Ecclesiastica*, he is called "disciple" of Peter at 2,15,1; "interpreter" at 3,39,14–15; and "disciple and interpreter" at 5,8,3.) Some ancient documents, such as the canon of Muratori, say Mark did not know Jesus or did not follow him in his earthly life, but all insist that he faithfully reproduced the preaching of Peter. The most ancient witness that we have is that of Papias of Hierapolis (60–130 A.D.) as quoted in the *Historia Ecclesiastica* (3,39,14–15).

> Mark, who was the interpreter of Peter, carefully put into writing, although without any order, what he recalled of what our Lord had said and done. He had not heard our Lord, nor followed him, but, as I said, later followed Peter, who imparted his teachings as needed and not as someone

compiling the sayings of the Lord. But, happily, Mark did not make any mistakes in writing things as he remembered them.

Similar statements can be found in St. Irenaeus ("Mark, the disciple and interpreter of Peter, also transmitted to us in writing what was preached by Peter." *Contra Haereses*, 3,1,1), and Clement of Alexandria:

> The Gospel according to Mark was begun in the following manner: When Peter was preaching the word in Rome and explaining the Gospel under the action of the Spirit, those who were present in great numbers on that occasion asked that Mark, because he had spent a long time accompanying Peter and recalled the things that he had said, put his words in writing. He did this and gave the Gospel to those who had asked him for it. When Peter heard about it, he did not say anything to hinder nor to promote it. (Eusebius of Caesarea, *Historia Ecclesiastica*, 6,14,5–7)

Who is this Mark? Traditionally he is identified as someone known to the earliest community whom 1 Peter 5:13 calls "my son." A Mark also appears in three Pauline letters (Philem 24; 2 Tim 4:11; Col 4:10). Colossians refers to him as "a cousin of Barnabas" and he therefore has been identified with that Mark whom Barnabas brought with him on an apostolic mission with Paul (Acts 12:25) and on another mission undertaken by Barnabas without Paul, after breaking with the latter over whether or not to bring Mark (Acts 15:36–39). This last text reports that he was called John Mark, and elsewhere (Acts 12:12) it is said that John Mark was the son of Mary, who received Peter into her house when he was freed from prison by an angel.

One can conclude from all of these references that the Mark to whom Papias refers is the same person mentioned so often in the New Testament. Some modern authors hold that imprecision in Mark's description of the geography and customs of Palestine argues against identifying the disciple of Peter and the Mark mentioned in Acts. According to the majority of scholars, however, the evidence for this hypothesis is not as persuasive as the evidence, internal and external to the Gospel, in support of the traditional view.

The Place and Date of Composition

Traditionally, Rome has always been thought to be the place where the Gospel of Mark was written.

This hypothesis is confirmed to some extent by indications in the text. Since the narrator explains Jewish customs, the work evidently is directed to people unfamiliar with the finer details of Judaism. The most extensive of the explanations is Mark 7:3–4: "For the Pharisees, and all the Jews, do not eat unless they wash their hands, observing the tradition of the elders; and when they come from the market place, they do not eat unless they purify themselves; and there are many other traditions which they observe, the washing of cups and pots and vessels of bronze." There are also brief explanatory interruptions: Mk 14:12 ("And on the first day of Unleavened Bread, when they sacrificed the Passover lamb") and Mk 15:42 ("It was the day of Preparation, that is, the day before the Sabbath").

On the other hand, the Gospel takes for granted Roman technical terms: "The soldiers led him away inside the palace (that is, the praetorium)" (Mk 15:16), "She put in two *leptas*, which is a *quadrante*," a Roman coin (Mk 12:42). It also translates Aramaic expressions used by Jesus. For example: "*Boanerges*, that is, sons of thunder" (Mk 3:17), "*Talitha qum* which means: 'little girl, I say to you, arise'" (Mk 3:41). Other examples appear in Mark 7:11, 14:36, 15:22, and 15:34.

Thus we may suppose that the audience of the second Gospel was not familiar with the Palestinian language and customs but did know Roman ways. Supporting the hypothesis are the presence of many Latinisms and turns of phrase more easily understood by a Roman audience. Although Latin words used by Mark—*speculator*, denarius, centurion, etc.—may have been in common use throughout the empire, other indications in the Gospel point to specifically Roman customs: for example, the manner of dividing the hours of the night (Mk 6:48; 13:35). Mark also mentions that Simon of Cyrene (Mk 14:21) was the father of Alexander and Rufus, persons known to the Christians of Rome (cf. Rom 16:13), etc.

Clearly then, Mark wrote for these Christians. Modern scholarship has not greatly affected this conclusion. Such new thinking as has emerged relates mainly to the internal study of the Gospel. A few authors (W. Marxen and H. C. Kee), basing themselves mainly on chapter 13, the eschatological discourse at the Temple, and the use of the word Galilee, think the second Gospel was composed in northern Palestine or southern Syria, and was directed to a community living in a pagan environment that had experienced persecution and the defection from the faith of some of its members; these people are supposed to be awaiting the abomination of desolation. These scholars place the time at about the year 67, when Roman troops have begun the conquest that in the year 70 would culminate in the destruction of Jerusalem. Mark's Latinisms are explained by the fact that, as Flavius Josephus attests, there were Roman enclaves in that area.

In general, the critical literature tends to agree that the reasoning of these authors does not require giving up the traditional view in favor of a new one. The factors to which they call attention, though undoubtedly present in the second Gospel, are quite well explained on the supposition that the text was composed in Rome shortly before the year 70.

In any case, the great majority of scholars agree on the relationship between the second Gospel and St. Peter. Some, but very few, have interpreted this relationship in a manner contrary to the traditional reading. Mark's attitude toward Peter and the twelve is said to be rather critical, since the Evangelist often records their incomprehension and weakness. For traditional critics, however, this is a sign of humility. Considering the unity of the early community and the influence upon it of the apostolic group, this seems the correct interpretation.

Given that the content of the Gospel of Mark is almost completely included in the other two synoptics, that many fewer ancient manuscripts of Mark are preserved than of the others, and that it is hardly commented on in catechesis, its link to Peter probably explains its inclusion in all the canonical lists.

2. Literary and Theological Characteristics

Critics usually sum up the literary characteristics of this Gospel by saying its writer had an imperfect style, but was an able narrator.

Literary style. A quick reading of the work makes it clear that Greek was not the author's native language. He was not a polished writer and at times he loses his way. His vocabulary is not excessively large, and his syntax is simple. Clauses and phrases often are strung together (parataxis) by conjunctions ("and"), prepositions ("for"), or adverbs ("then"). Sometimes tenses jump back and forth without warning within the same passage.

Narrative style. In its simplicity, nevertheless, Mark's writing has great vividness. He has the gift of making his story live. He makes constant use of the historical present—"he comes," "he says," "they go," occurring more than 150 times—and provides a minute description of details and circumstances that Matthew and Luke narrate abstractly.[1] When referring to Jesus and his disciples, he often uses the third person plural—"then they arrived, they saw, they went," etc.[2]— where the other Evangelists use the first person, referring only to Jesus: "then he arrived with his disciples. . . ." The narrative becomes so vivid in these cases that one can imagine the voice of an eyewitness saying repeatedly, "we arrived, we saw. . . ."

No doubt such characteristics reflect the lively style of St. Peter's accounts. But they also are related to the message of the Gospel. Mark's vivid and passionate manner helps transport us to the small cities on the shore of the Lake of Gennesaret, makes us feel the crowding of the people who followed Jesus and see the gestures of Christ—in a word, enter into the Gospel story as if we were participants. This dramatic quality may explain why the miracles have so large a place in the text. On the other hand, unlike the other Gospels, there are no long discourses. More than the other Evangelists, St. Mark says that Jesus "taught"; but he provides little evidence of the teachings of Jesus, at least in the form of long discourses. Indeed, there are only two of these: the parables (Mk 4:1–34) and the eschatological discourse (Mk 13:1–37).

In my view, these features correspond to aspects of the Gospel message highlighted more in Mark than in either of the other two synoptics: (1) the Gospel, (2) the discovery

---

1. Cf. the cure of the paralytic, Mk 2:1–12, compared with Mt 9:18 and Lk 5:17–26; that of the possessed man in Gerasa, Mk 5:1–20, compared with Mt 8:28–34 and Lk 8:26–39; etc. Some small details are only referred to by St. Mark: that, during the tempest on the lake, Jesus was sleeping on a "pillow" in the stern of the boat (Mk 4:38); that the sons of Zebedee were called "sons of thunder" by our Lord (Mk 3:17); that the blind man of Jericho was named Bartimaeus (Mk 10:46), etc.

2. Cf. Mk 1:21, 29; 3:20; 5:1, 38; 6:53–54; 8:22; 9:14, 30, 33; 10:32, 46; 11:1, 12, 15, 20, 27; 14:18, 22, 26, 32.

of the identity of Jesus (at times this is called the mystery of Jesus or the messianic secret), and (3) the universality of his mission.

The Gospel

Among the Evangelists, Mark makes most frequent use— eight times in all—of the word "gospel" used in a categorical sense. In addition, at the very start of his narrative—"The beginning of the Gospel of Jesus Christ, the Son of God"—he seems to indicate that this is the subject he means to deal with. To understand that, we have to recall certain things.

Where the other Evangelists use expressions like "the Gospel of the kingdom," St. Mark says simply "the Gospel." In this he is like St. Paul, who more than fifty times uses the word categorically. In these two cases, Paul and Mark, the meaning seems clear: *The word Gospel sums up the person and the work of Jesus Christ.*

Etymologically, "gospel" means good news. In Homer and in Plutarch the word, used in plural, refers to the reward given to one who brings good auguries or to the sacrifice of thanksgiving offered for such auguries to the gods. In the Old Testament, gospel has a simple, everyday sense: for example, news of a victory over enemies. In two places, however, the prophet Isaiah uses "to evangelize" to express the good news of the Messianic times, when God would save his people: "How beautiful upon the mountains are the feet of him who *brings good tidings*, who publishes peace, who *brings good tidings* of good, who publishes salvation, who says to Zion, 'Your God reigns'" (Is 52:7); "The Spirit of the Lord GOD is upon me, because the LORD has anointed me *to bring good tidings* to the afflicted" (Is 61:1). In addition, one instance of a pagan use of the word is of interest. Found on an inscription in Priene (Asia Minor) dedicated to Augustus and dating from 9 B.C., it says: "The day of the birth of god has signaled the beginning of good news for the world."

Jesus, in proclaiming the Gospel, announced that his actions fulfilled the promises of salvation announced by God. In St. Mark, one finds a radicalization of the meaning: the Gospel, the good news for mankind, is not the birth of Augustus; it is Jesus, who by his deeds has obtained salvation for us.

What, more precisely, is the content and purpose of the Gospel? In considering that question, we need to examine the passages where the word appears.

1. "The beginning of the Gospel of Jesus Christ, the Son of God." (Mk 1:1)

2. "Now after John was arrested, Jesus came into Galilee, preaching the Gospel of God, and saying, 'The time is fulfilled, and the kingdom of God is at hand; repent, and believe in the Gospel.'" (Mk 1:14–15)

3. "For whoever would save his life will lose it; and whoever loses his life for my sake and the Gospel's will save it." (Mk 8:35)

4. "There is no one who has left house or brothers or sisters or mother or father or children or lands, for my sake and for the Gospel, who will not receive . . ." (Mk 10:29–30)

5. "And the Gospel must first be preached to all nations." (Mk 13:10)

6. "And truly, I say to you, wherever the Gospel is preached in the whole world, what she has done will be told in memory of her." (Mk 14:9)

7. "And he said to them, 'Go into all the world and preach the Gospel to the whole creation.'" (Mk 16:15)

As the second text (Mk 1:14–15) indicates, the Gospel is first of all the work of Christ, what Jesus Christ preached and did. Therefore, the reason for the Gospel, as indicated in the third and fourth texts (Mk 8:35; 10:29), is the same—Jesus: to give one's life for the Gospel is to give it for Jesus. This Gospel, the work of Jesus, should be preached in the whole world, as the fifth and seventh texts indicate (Mk 13:10; 16:15). In the sixth text (Mk 14:9)—the words of Jesus upon being anointed by the woman of Bethany—these ideas are implied. It is also part of the Gospel to consider who Jesus truly is and react to him.

St. Mark's intention should by now be clear: he is fulfilling the command of Jesus to preach the Gospel. He does so in a vivid, impassioned way. Seeing so clearly the actions of Christ and the reactions of others, the reader is swept up in the narrative and he also reacts.

These reflections illuminate most of the stylistic devices noted above: the historical present, the rapidity of the narrative—almost everything occurs "at once"—the emotional evaluation of persons, etc. We read St. Mark "as spectators of the events, for the Evangelist seeks to place us in the presence of the Gospel—Jesus active in the world—and we must take a stand in regard to him.

This feature of the Gospel is closely related to the one we consider next.

The Mystery of Jesus and its Discovery by Mankind

Several things in the Gospel of St. Mark are surprising at first and perhaps difficult to understand.

1. Jesus' repeated prohibition of revealing his identity or publicizing his miracles. Among those to whom prohibitions are directed are devils, those cured, and the disciples.

2. The fact that the parables, and other sayings of our Lord, are delivered in obscure language that needs interpretation. The Gospel for this reason often recounts a privileged explanation provided by our Lord to his disciples alone.

3. The impression that, despite this special instruction, the disciples did not understand Jesus. This lack of understanding on the disciples' part seems to complement the emphasis on not divulging Jesus' identity.

William Wrede, a German exegete of the early twentieth century, considered these features to form part of what he called "the Messianic secret." According to Wrede's theory, St. Mark was not just an ingenuous chronicler of the life of Jesus, as many had believed up to then, but a consummate writer. As Wrede would have it, Jesus did not do the Messianic works attributed to him in the Gospel. After his death, however, his disciples claimed that he had done these things, while forbidding them to speak of them; Mark, supposedly, is a masterful practitioner of this deception, which allowed the apostles to preach Jesus as Messiah and explained why his deeds nevertheless were not well known in his lifetime.

This hypothesis is rejected today for many reasons. It can be shown that Jesus proclaimed himself as Messiah and died for doing so, that he performed miracles, etc. Still, the disconcerting facts noted above remain, especially the command of silence. Here we need to reflect on two distinct factors: Jesus' attitude and the way Mark's Gospel depicts it.

1. **Jesus' attitude.** The command of silence—which those who receive it often disobey—is a feature of all of the Gospels, although in John it is expressed differently. Scholars agree that Jesus wished to revise the concept of Messianism held by people in his time, and express it in terms more like those referring to the Servant of the Lord described in the Book of Isaiah. This conclusion is derived from other elements of the Gospel—for instance, use of "Son of Man"—but the command of silence is consistent with it.

2. **How Mark presents the command.** There are various commands of silence in this Gospel: to the devils, to men, to the disciples.

    a. It is reasonable to suppose that Jesus enjoined silence upon the devils who recognized him (Mk 1:24–25, 34, 3:12), because he did not want their testimony.

b. After some miracles, Jesus asked those who had benefited to remain silent about what had happened. These were a leper (Mk 1:44), a person raised from the dead (Mk 5:43), a deaf person (Mk 7:36), and a blind man (Mk 8:26). Two factors should be noted. First, after the episode involving the blind man, St. Peter confesses Jesus to be the Messiah. Second, these four miracles practically coincide with the Messianic signs cited by Jesus to the disciples of the Baptist that he is the Messiah: "Go and tell John what you hear and see: the blind receive their sight and the lame walk, lepers are cleansed and the deaf hear, and the dead are raised up, and the poor have good news preached to them" (Mt 11:4–5; cf. Lk 7:18–23). Reasoning from the evidence of these signs may well have moved Peter to confess Jesus as the Messiah.

c. Jesus acknowledged the title of Messiah given him by Peter, but immediately ordered his disciples not to divulge it (Mk 8:30). Shortly after, following the Transfiguration, he repeated a similar prohibition—referring to his divine Sonship (Mk 9:9)—to those who witnessed the miracle. In short, Jesus is the Christ and Son of God, and Peter knows this.

The conclusion from all this is relatively obvious. St. Mark tells of the acts and words of Christ that lead people who witness them to confess that he is the Messiah; but Jesus does not want them to reach this conclusion too quickly, since his mission as Messiah is not understood apart from the mystery of the Cross. In the light of the Cross, one grasps that Jesus is not only the Christ but also, as the centurion who saw him die affirmed, the Son of God. Here is the mystery of Jesus in its totality.

Mark's Gospel tells its story from the disciples' point of view. He shows how Jesus' followers saw what he did and were moved to confess him as what he is. Following the same path, those who read the Gospel now can do the same.

To be Messiah and Son of God, and yet suffer, is only one dimension of the mystery of Jesus. The command of silence also reflects certain other circumstances, especially lack of understanding of what the Lord taught and did. This failure of comprehension among the disciples arises from the same source: the mystery of Jesus must be understood as a whole—one should not leap to conclusions under pressure.

This is the context of expressions in Mark 4:10–12 that have often been a problem for interpreters:

> And when he was alone, those who were about him with the twelve asked him concerning the parables. And he said to them, "To you has been given the secret of the kingdom of God, but for those outside everything is in parables; so that *they may indeed see but not perceive, and may indeed hear but not understand; lest they should turn again, and be forgiven.*"

The words of Isaiah (6:9–10) pronounced here by our Lord appear six times in the New Testament. In relation to the first evangelization, they explain why many Jews who were Christ's contemporaries did not recognize him as Messiah; and in Mark's Gospel they underline the mystery of the kingdom of God that Christ revealed. His teaching was not esoteric—on the contrary, it was to spread throughout the world, and, precisely as universal, it must be understood. Therefore he explained it to his disciples. At the same time, nevertheless, someone who wishes to understand Christ must do so "from within"—with the desire to understand.

This universal destination of the Gospel also is an important theme of the second Gospel, whose literary features are mingled with its teachings.

The Universality of Our Lord's Mission

In one way or another all of the Gospels seek to explain that, even though the earthly mission of Jesus Christ took place among Jews, its scope was universal. The Gospel of St. John (Jn 12:20–36) calls attention to this in an episode in which some "Greeks" want to meet Jesus and the Lord then teaches that the glorification of the Son of Man must come first. Each of the other Gospels has its own way of making this point. Besides the three texts noted above in which Jesus calls for the Gospel to be preached throughout the world, to all peoples, St. Mark's Gospel stresses this universality of the mission through the gestures of Jesus and the implications the Evangelist draws from them.

A notable feature of this Gospel is its repeated use of the name *Galilee*. Jesus crosses Galilee continually; the Lake of Gennesaret is frequently called the Sea of Galilee, and the Lord goes from Galilee to nearby regions, etc. Galilee is where Jesus begins his public ministry and carries out the major part of it; it is also where he announces the new beginning after his resurrection (Mk 14:28; 16:7). But from a social point of view, Galilee is above all a crossroads of peoples and cultures—the Rome of Palestine, one might say. Even though Jesus' earthly ministry was confined to Israel, he suggests by his labors in Galilee (and Mark emphasizes) that what he did was directed ultimately to all mankind.

Although he worked in Galilee, Jesus was approached by people from all the neighboring areas. The third chapter of St. Mark says:

> Jesus withdrew with his disciples to the sea, and a great multitude from Galilee followed; also from Judea and Jerusalem and Idumea and from beyond the Jordan and from about Tyre and Sidon. (Mk 3:7–9)

Moreover, Jesus himself went back and forth in Palestine. Precisely because Galilee stood at a crossroads with pagan lands, he acted in those lands, too. The episode of the possessed man of Gerasa is very significant. That this was pagan territory is clear from the herd of swine present there.

Jesus did not allow the man who was cured to follow him, but instead sent him to his family and friends to announce (the same verb used here as at the end of the Gospel, where it designates the apostolic mission Jesus entrusts to his disciples) that the mercy of God has reached them, too. And this the man who had been cured proclaims throughout the entire Decapolis.

But the most significant treatment of the universality of Jesus' mission occurs in the cluster passages between the two multiplications of the loaves, usually called "the section of the loaves" (Mk 6:30–8:10). Here we consider only the principal points. In the first multiplication of loaves, Jesus shows himself as the Messiah king who convokes the people in the desert, feeds them with the words of his preaching, and offers them a Messianic banquet. Clearly this is a symbol of the Church, the new People of God, to whom our Lord offers physical food and the spiritual food of his teaching. On the other hand, in the second multiplication of the loaves the people are said to have come from "afar"—a word frequently used in the New Testament to designate the Gentiles (Acts 2:39; 22:21; Eph 2:13, 17)—and that Jesus used "seven" loaves and "seven" bushel baskets were left over, as opposed to the "twelve" baskets before (cf. 6:43). Between the two multiplications, Jesus goes to the pagan territories of Tyre and Sidon, and there his dialogue with the Syrophoenician woman takes place. Let us look at this passage.

> And from there he arose and went away to the region of Tyre and Sidon. And he entered a house, and would not have any one know it; yet he could not be hid. But immediately a woman, whose little daughter was possessed by an unclean spirit, heard of him, and came and fell down at his feet. Now the woman was a Greek, a Syrophoenician by birth. And she begged him to cast the demon out of her daughter. And he said to her, "Let the children first be fed, for it is not right to take the children's bread

and throw it to the dogs." But she answered him, "Yes, Lord; yet even the dogs under the table eat the children's crumbs." And he said to her, "For this saying you may go your way; the demon has left your daughter." And she went home, and found the child lying in bed, and the demon gone. (Mk 7:24–30)

The episode shows in a symbolic way that Jesus' mission was directed first to Israel (the children) and afterwards to all mankind. This is the meaning of the passages that fall between the two multiplications of loaves: salvation, directed first of all to Israel, is addressed to all peoples.

More could be said, but it appears to me that these themes—Jesus as the Good News, the discovery of his identity, his universal mission—sum up the most important features of Mark.

3. Structure of the Gospel

In considering the structure of a Gospel, its design, one points to features that make it possible to situate each passage—in this case, each episode—in the whole. The structure of St. Mark is more or less as follows.

First Part: The Ministry of Jesus in Galilee

Jesus spoke to all of the people, and showed who he was with deeds and words. The people asked themselves who he was ("Who is this?" cf. Mk 1:27; 2:7, 12; 3:32; 4:41; 6:2, 14–16, 40; 8:27–28), without getting an answer until Peter confessed him to be the Messiah (Mk 8:29).

Second Part: Ministry on the Way to Jerusalem and in Jerusalem

Jesus directed himself principally to his disciples, teachings them about his position as Servant of God who would give his life for mankind. After the fulfillment of those teachings, the account concludes with the centurion's confession that he was the Son of God (Mk 15:39) and with the resurrection.

One can also outline a similar structure from the perspective of the narrative scheme. It would go more or less as follows.

The first verse sums up the Gospel. Mark says who Jesus is: the Messiah and the Son of God. But this reality has two dimensions: the manifestation of Jesus as such and the discovery of that reality by human beings. From this point of view, the Gospel has two parts, clearly divided by the confession of Peter at Caesarea Philippi (Mk 8:29). Until then, Jesus by his words—directed to the people, often to crowds—and with his works, showed who he was; but neither the disciples nor the people in general seemed able to comprehend his identity (cf. Mk 1:27; 2:7, 12; 3:32; 4:41; 6:2, 14–16, etc.). At Caesarea Philippi, Peter confesses him to be the Messiah, and immediately Jesus begins to impart a special teaching—directed above all to the disciples—instructing them how they should think of him in his capacity as Messiah: not as a political liberator, but as the Son of Man who must suffer affronts to the Servant of God even to the extent of death, and afterwards rise. Almost at the end of the Gospel, at the foot of the cross, a Gentile, the Roman centurion, declares Jesus to be the Son of God. Thus he has indeed been recognized under the two titles identified by the Evangelist at the start.

Other aspects in the account emphasize the relation between the truth about Jesus and what people discover. For example, as the narrative proceeds it is observable that a confession of Christ by men is followed by a manifestation from heaven confirming and perfecting it: the declaration of John the Baptist is followed by the voice from heaven at the Baptism of Jesus; the confession of Peter at the Transfiguration is followed by a voice from heaven; the words of the centurion at the foot of the cross are followed by those of the young man who announces the resurrection (cf. Mk 1:7 with Mk 11:11; Mk 8:29 with Mk 9:7; Mk 15:39 with Mk 16:5–6).

The structure of the Gospel reinforces its message and underlying purpose. Jesus' works are presented in an order that invites one to ask who he is and to respond with complete faith: He is the Christ, the Son of God.

4. Principle Contents

If one reads with attention, one can find the whole Christian message expressed explicitly or implicitly in each of the Gospels. St. Mark provides the basis for the doctrine of the sacraments, grace, piety, norms of conduct, etc. Its principal contents are those features found throughout the narrative or else given greater emphasis than they receive in the other Gospels. Two motifs stand out in this regard.

Jesus Christ

Jesus Christ is described in the Gospel in his divine and his human condition. His identity as the Son of God is affirmed a number of times, above all by the voice of the Father (Mk 1:11; 9:7) but also by Jesus himself before Caiphas (Mk 14:62), leading to his being condemned to death. He is also the Messiah, but a Messiah Son of God manifesting his status through his mission as the Servant of God who gives his life on the cross in fulfillment of the Scriptures. As Messiah and Son of God, Jesus has power, authority (*exousia*)—a word that, together with the word Gospel, is the second motif in St. Mark. Jesus has power and manifests it: power over demons, power over the Sabbath, power to forgive sins, power to raise the dead, etc.

But even more characteristic of St. Mark may be the theme of Jesus' true humanity: against any form of docetism, Mark emphasizes that our Lord is true man. Jesus who sleeps in the stern of the boat (Mk 4:3), is saddened by the lack of faith of his neighbors at Nazareth (Mk 6:6), trembles

(Mk 7:38; 8:12), has compassion (Mk 1:41), becomes angry at his disciples (Mk 10:3), is afflicted and feels anguish when praying in the garden (Mk 14:36). Consider, for instance, the various "looks" of our Lord recorded by Mark.

> And he looked around at them with anger, grieved at their hardness of heart, and said to the man . . ." (Mk 3:5)

> And looking around on those who sat about him . . . (Mk 3:34)

> And he looked around to see who had done it . . . (Mk 5:32)

> But turning and seeing his disciples, he rebuked Peter, and said . . . (Mk 8:33)

> And Jesus looking upon him loved him. (Mk 10:21)

> And Jesus looked around and said to his disciples . . . (Mk 10:23)

> Jesus looked at them and said, "With men it is impossible, but not with God; for all things are possible with God." (Mk 10:27)

> And he sat down opposite the treasury, and watched the multitude putting money into the treasury. Many rich people put in large sums. (Mk 12:41)

In concluding this section, let us recall the episode of Jesus with the children in chapter ten:

> And they were bringing children to him, that he might touch them; and the disciples rebuked them. But when Jesus saw it he was indignant, and said to them, "Let the children come to me, do not hinder them; for to such belongs the kingdom of God. Truly, I say to you, whoever does not receive the kingdom of God like a child shall not enter it." And he took them in his arms and blessed them, laying his hands upon them. (Mk 10:13–16)

Like the other Evangelists, Mark recalls Jesus' teaching about spiritual childhood as necessary for entering the Kingdom of God. But the spontaneity and liveliness of his treatment highlight the humanity of our Lord, including his anger at the disciples who did not understand him.

This points to another theme that occurs often in the second Gospel: Jesus' disciples and what being a disciple means.

The Disciples

The Gospel records attitudes toward Jesus: of the people, of the authorities, of the women, of the disciples. In this connection, the account of the condemnation of Jesus and the denials of Peter is a virtual compendium of Mark's Gospel. We quote only a few paragraphs here.

And they led Jesus to the high priest; and all the chief priests and the elders and the scribes were assembled. And Peter had followed him at a distance, right into the courtyard of the high priest; and he was sitting with the guards, and warming himself at the fire.

Now the chief priests and the whole council sought testimony against Jesus to put him to death; but they found none. . . . But he was silent and made no answer. Again the high priest asked him, "Are you the Christ, the Son of the Blessed?" And Jesus said, "I am; and you will see the Son of man seated at the right hand of Power, and coming with the clouds of heaven." And the high priest tore his garments, and said, "Why do we still need witnesses? You have heard his blasphemy. What is your decision?" And they all condemned him as deserving death. . . .

And as Peter was below in the courtyard, one of the maids of the high priest came; and seeing Peter warming himself, she looked at him, and said, "You also were with the Nazarene, Jesus." But he denied it, saying, "I neither know nor understand what you mean." . . . And immediately the cock crowed a second time. And Peter remembered how Jesus had said to him, "Before the cock crows twice, you will deny me three times." And he broke down and wept. (Mk 14:53–72)

The Evangelist speaks of Jesus and Peter in the two first verses. Then he depicts a scene with two distinct, contrasting actions: Jesus is falsely accused, confesses the truth, and for that is condemned to death by the high priest and mocked by the servants; Peter is accused of something which is true, but he denies Jesus with a lie and gets off safely when the maid accuses him. In the end, nevertheless, he weeps, making it clear that Peter's greatness is not in his fortitude but his contrition.

The passage illustrates not only the authorities' fury toward Jesus but also his relations with his disciples. It will be sufficient here to recall the principal characteristics.

1. In Mark, Jesus is always with his disciples. The first action of his public life is to summon them to follow him. Later he calls Matthew. By the third chapter, the twelve have been assembled. Mark says:

   > [He] called to him those whom he desired; and they
   > came to him. And he appointed twelve, to be with
   > him, and to be sent out to preach and have authority
   > to cast out demons. (Mk 3:13–15)

   This statement is elaborated and illustrated in the Gospel as a whole. Throughout, "the twelve" is used almost as a synonym for "disciples." They are always with him—we never see our Lord alone in his ministry. The disciples are called *mathetes*, students, because they are learning from him. It is said repeatedly that they follow (*akolouthousin*) Jesus. This following is understood in a double sense: physical, because they follow him here and there, and spiritual, because they follow his way of life. Our Lord has chosen them to be sent out, to be apostles, and therefore communicates his power to them. The Gospel emphasizes the continuity between the mission of the apostles and his mission. This is why they are privileged recipients of Jesus' teaching (Mk 4:10–34; 7:1–23; 8:27–10:45; 13:1–37), unique witnesses of his acts of power (Mk 4:35–41; 5:37–43), of the Transfiguration (Mk 9:2–13); it is why they accompany him at the Last Supper and help him in the multiplication of the loaves.

2. At the same time, the disciples share the failure to understand Jesus of many persons in the Gospel. This failure of understanding affects his teaching and also some of his actions. This is evident on nearly every page of the Gospel. Not only do they misunderstand him, they also abandon him and deny him. We read more than once that Judas, who betrayed him, was "one of the twelve" (Mk 14:10, 20, 43).

Some authors say this double aspect of the disciples is emphasized in Mark because his Gospel, written in Rome after the persecution of Nero, sought to encourage weak Christians who had fallen; they failed to grasp that to follow Christ meant being faced with the cross, having to begin again, and not to shrink from speaking out like the frightened women who fell silent after the angel told them Jesus had risen. His message to us all is that, even in our weaknesses, the resurrected Christ has called us, his disciples, to continue his mission.

It would be possible to say much more, but what has been said calls attention to matters central to appreciating the Gospel of St. Mark. As is the advice of St. Josemaría Escrivá: in reading the Gospel place oneself imaginatively in its scenes "as one more person."

6

The Gospel According to St. Luke

Juan Luis Caballero

1. AUTHOR, PLACE, AND DATE OF COMPOSITION

The Author

Like the other Gospels, the third Gospel does not include the name of its author in the text, but tradition from the beginning has attributed it to Luke, a companion of St. Paul. A very early text, the Bodmer XIV (P73) papyrus, dated between the years 175–225, is titled *Euangelion kata Loukan*, thus indicating its author. In the second century there are many patristic testimonies: St. Irenaeus in his *Contra Haereses*, 3,1, the *Prologo griego antimarcionita*, Tertullian, Origen, etc. The Muratorian fragment, a Christian document from the years 170–180, says:

> The third book of the Gospel is according to Luke. This Luke was a physician. Paul took him as his deputy because of his legal knowledge, and he wrote with his consent what he considered good. Nevertheless, he did not see the Lord in his mortal flesh. As a consequence, according to the information he was able to obtain, he began to speak from the birth of John (the Baptist).

St. Jerome, writing around the year 400, gathers these opinions and sums them up in his book *On Illustrious Men:*

> Luke, an Antiochean physician, with a good knowledge of Greek, as his writing demonstrates, follower and traveling companion of the apostle Paul, wrote a Gospel.

But who is this Luke, the disciple of Paul? In the New
tament this name appears on three occasions: Col 4:14; Phil
24; 2 Tim 4:11. In each case, Luke is a collaborator of St. Paul.
Colossians says in addition that he was a physician and was
numbered among the disciples who did not come from the
circumcision, in other words, he was of Gentile origin.

There also are many indications in the Gospel itself and
in the Acts of the Apostles. The author was not an eyewitness
of the ministry of Jesus (Lk 1:2), he is not of Palestinian origin, he is an educated person, as one can see especially from
texts like the prologue to the Gospel (though he respects the
simplicity of the older sources he uses), his language and doctrine have resemblances to the Pauline texts, and he knows
the Christian community of Antioch well.

Most visible to the reader perhaps is this writer's lack
of knowledge of Palestine. He is imprecise and often confused about geography, unaware that in Palestine the dead
were not buried in coffins (see the raising of the son of the
widow of Nain, Lk 7:14), ignorant of the fact that only
the fig tree, not other trees, shows signs of the beginning of
spring (Lk 21:29), etc.

In sum, the author of the third Gospel was a Christian of
the second generation, of pagan origin, probably from Antioch of Syria, educated, with a special interest in history, and
a disciple and companion of St. Paul.

The Place of Composition

According to tradition, the Gospel of Luke was written after
those of Matthew and Mark. The words of the prologue tend
to support this ("Inasmuch as many have undertaken to com-
pile a narrative of the things which have been accomplished
among us"). It was written in Corinth (Achaia, Greece), one
of the first centers of Christian expansion.

The Gospel is directed to a Christian named Theophilus.
It is not known whether this is a generic name—it means

"beloved of God"[1]—or that of a specific person. That Luke calls him "distinguished Theophilus," the same title St. Paul uses to address Festus (Acts 26:25), suggests that he is an illustrious person, one of those who, as Seneca tells us (*De tranquilitate animae* 9:4), in those times had baths and private libraries in their homes.

However that may be, Luke, like the other Evangelists, clearly had in view a more general audience made up of those Christians who want certain knowledge about the basis for what they have been taught. Clearly, too, these people are Christians of the Hellenistic world who do not know Palestine. This is evident from some significant details of his account, especially when compared with the other synoptics.

> **For example**
>
> St. Luke sometimes replaces Palestinian details with Hellenistic ones. The lowering of the paralytic by ropes in Capernaum provides an example. In Mark, the men simply "removed the roofing" (Mk 2:4), which would have been of wood and straw; but Luke, thinking of a Greek house, says the paralytic was let down from the flat roof "through the tiles" (Lk 5:17). Similar instances can be found elsewhere (cf. Lk 6:46–49).

The Date of Composition

To determine the date of composition, we must turn to the Acts of the Apostles, written by the same author (cf. Acts 1:1–2) since he says that he wrote the Gospel earlier. Acts ends with St. Paul a prisoner in Rome. This was his first imprisonment, at the beginning of the sixties. St. Paul later was freed, but Luke say nothing about this, pointing to the conclusion that the book was written while St. Paul was a prisoner, that is, around the year 63 at the latest. Beyond that, however,

---

1. From the grammatical point of view, it could also be translated as "he who loves God," although, properly speaking, "he who loves God" should be Philotheo.

the Acts of the Apostles ends where it makes theological sense to end, for at this point the words of our Lord opening the book are fulfilled: "You shall be my witnesses . . . to the ends of the earth." If this hypothesis is accepted, the date could accord with the purpose of the book. Luke writes to someone (Theophilus) who lacked access to those who were "eyewitnesses and ministers of the word," that is to say, the apostles and others of their generation, in order to supply order and exactitude. That situates us in the second Christian generation, around the years 70–80.

2. LITERARY AND THEOLOGICAL CHARACTERISTICS

Literary Style

No one who reads the third Gospel can help but be deeply impressed by its prologue.

> Inasmuch as many have undertaken to compile a narrative of the things which have been accomplished among us, just as they were delivered to us by those who from the beginning were eyewitnesses and ministers of the word, it seemed good to me also, having followed all things closely for some time past, to write an orderly account for you, most excellent Theophilus, that you may know the truth concerning the things of which you have been informed. (Lk 1:1–4)

The Greek of this passage is that of an educated person with a cultivated style and a broad vocabulary who uses words precisely. Greek clearly is his native language, and he was a good reader. As St. Jerome says (*Epistle* 19), Luke is "*graeci sermonis eruditissimus*"—very erudite in his use of Greek.

More important, however, is the purpose disclosed in these lines. Following the Greek model, the prologue briefly states the subject, sources, method, and purpose of the work. The *subject* is "the things which have been accomplished among us"—everything relating to Jesus and the origin and expansion of the early Church (bearing in mind that the Acts of the Apostles completes Luke's account). The *sources* are the eyewitnesses and the ministers of the word, that is to say, a well-established tradition and other books already written (presumably Matthew and Mark). His *method* is historical and literary, since he is giving detailed information about facts, but expressed in his own way. His *purpose* is to enable people to know with certainty the deeds and teachings underlying Christian faith.

The prologue calls implicit attention to facts that help one understand the composition of the Gospel. Luke is composing a "narration," which places his writing in the genre of history. In fact, he is a historian, as is corroborated by his references to secular history and to chronological dates (Lk 1:5; 2:1; 3:1–1, 23). Luke writes *in an orderly way* (Lk 1:3) because he judges that others had already written without much order. Besides, he was speaking of things that had taken place, had really happened, had "witnesses," and had been transmitted. Thus, Luke reflected the faith of the earlier tradition, which was based on real events. Luke manifests great fidelity to his sources. He had traveled, knew personally people and places, and so could be more precise in what he wrote.

In St. Luke the order of the narrative and the perspective he wishes to give to the message are closely related. As historian and theologian, he chooses and arranges data according to the points he wishes to make. Even details of style reflect this. Let us consider two, relating to fidelity to sources and discipleship.

Fidelity to the sources. The Greek of Luke's Gospel is notably correct by comparison with the other Gospels and is marked by careful grammar; the translation of Hebrew, Aramaic, and Latin terms, and the substitution of genteel expressions for common ones. Still, when transcribing the words of Jesus, he preserves Semitisms, including syntax, and thus shows his fidelity to his sources. This bolsters confidence in his writings as a reliable basis for belief.

The disciple of Christ. In this Gospel one can often glimpse the cultivated Greek concerned for *doxa*, good opinion, in reference to the decorousness of what he relates. So, for example, unlike the other synoptics, he says nothing about the garb and food of John the Baptist. The others do: "Now John wore a garment of camel's hair, and a leather girdle around his waist; and his food was locusts and wild honey" (Mt 3:4; Mk 1:6). So, too, the description of the possessed man of Gerasa. Mark supplies details of violent and bizarre behavior. Luke merely says that "for a long time he had worn no clothes, and he lived not in a house but among the tombs. . . . He was kept under guard, and bound with chains and fetters, but he broke the bonds and was driven by the demon into the desert" (Lk 8:26, 29).

This decorum suggests sensitivity to public opinion. St. Luke records a parable about people who took the best places at a banquet, then shamefacedly had to give them up (Lk 14:7–11), even as a man who chose the poorer place but was invited to go higher was "honored in the presence of all" (Lk 14:10). He recalls Jesus' admonition that someone who leaves all in order to follow him must be careful to persevere, lest "not able to finish, all who see it begin to mock him" (Lk 14:29).

Paradoxically, however, Luke phrases the last Beatitude in this way: "Woe to you, when all men speak well of you" (Lk 6:26). He also records numerous insults to Christ and is the only Gospel writer who tells of the coming and going of the bound Christ between Pilate and Herod. Only he speaks of the insults in the third announcement of the Passion: "He will be delivered to the Gentiles, and will be mocked and shamefully treated and spit upon; they will scourge him and kill him, and on the third day he will rise" (Lk 18:32–33).

Hence this paradox: Luke loves order, an open spirit, clarity; but his model is Christ, and knowing that Jesus suffered insults, being spat upon, affronts of all kinds, he knows also that this will be the path of the Christian who wishes to follow his Master.

We shall return to this teaching of Luke. Now, however, let us consider other aspects of his Gospel.

Theological Characteristics

History and the history of salvation. The history Luke writes has a very specific purpose: to present the *story of salvation*, from the Incarnation to the spread of the Gospel among the Gentiles. Both Luke's Gospel and the Acts of the Apostles tell of the salvific action of God in history. That the theme of salvation is fundamental is evident from the number of times he uses the word (cf. Lk 1:47, 69, 71, 77; 2:11, 30; 3:6; 19:9). Salvation as St. Luke treats it is found not only in the death and resurrection of Christ, but also in later events—the Ascension of Christ into heaven and the evangelization that follows (cf. Acts 13:47; 28:28). Indeed, in the Acts salvation is completed with the coming of the Holy Spirit, who provides the impetus for the spread of the Gospel throughout the world.

The place of the Holy City. In Luke, Jerusalem has a central role. The infancy of Jesus begins and ends in the Temple, the temptations in the desert end in Jerusalem. From the beginning of his public life, Jesus commences *to walk* toward Jerusalem, where the events of salvation culminate (Lk 9:51–53: "When the days drew near for him to be received up, he set his face to go to Jerusalem. And he sent messengers ahead of him, who went and entered a village of the Samaritans, to make ready for him; but the people would not receive him, because his face was set toward Jerusalem"). The apparitions of the risen Jesus described by Luke are not those of Galilee but Jerusalem. The Gospel closes in the Temple (Lk 24:43: "and [they] were continually in the temple blessing God").

Jerusalem is the site of salvation's culmination not only because our Lord died there but above all because it is the site of his *Ascension*, the final stage toward which Jesus traveled. The Ascension is the end of his earthly life (Lk 24:51–53), the passage from the Resurrection to glory (Acts 1:6–11), from which he sends the Holy Spirit.

Conclusion. This conjunction of times and places expresses the motives guiding the work of St. Luke. It could be summed up in a phrase of Jesus standing at the center of the Gospel: "The law and the prophets were until John; since then the good news of the kingdom of God is preached, and every one enters it violently" (Lk 16:16). God was preparing a people, with the intention of sending his Son and, through him, extending salvation to all mankind.

3. THE STRUCTURE OF THE GOSPEL

Luke narrates the ministry of Jesus in three parts: Galilee, the ascent to Jerusalem, Jerusalem. These coincide with the other synoptics (except that Jesus' going up to Jerusalem is much longer in Luke than in Matthew and Mark). The ministry of Jesus is preceded by a prologue and some chapters—a singular feature of this Gospel—speaking of the origins of Jesus, of his infancy, and of his preparation for the public life. In the journey up to Jerusalem (ten chapters in Luke, against only two or three in Matthew and Mark) he emphasizes especially that Jesus was directing his salvific message to all men and women.

The Presentation

The prologue (Lk 1:1–4, 13) states the intention of the work. It is followed by the first great episode of the third Gospel (Lk 1:5–2:52), in which the author speaks of the infancy of Jesus. In Matthew, the episodes on the infancy are a conceptual summary of the Gospel: they say who Jesus is from practically all points of view. In Luke these 111 verses are, as it were, the Old Testament's final chapter and the New Testament's first. Here we are told who Jesus is: the Messiah, the Savior. With him is his mother, who also has a central role in the plan of salvation.

Luke also tells of Jesus' preparation for his public ministry (Lk 3:1–4, 13). He emphasizes the outreach of the salvation accomplished by Christ, organizing the treatment around three motifs: John the Baptist, the temptations of Jesus, and Jesus' genealogy.

First Part: The Ministry of Jesus in Galilee

Here Jesus' mission is capsulized (Lk 4:16–30) and the beginning of his ministry is described: his preaching, and the choice, formation, and sending forth of the disciples and apostles on their mission. After an account of the beginnings of the ministry of Jesus (Lk 4:14–6:11), Luke tells of his miracles and activity in Galilee (Lk 6:12–8:56). Finally, he centers on the travel of Jesus with his apostles (Lk 9:1–50). He sets the Sermon on the level place (Lk 6:17–49) and the parables of the Kingdom (Lk 8:4–18) are presented as central to his preaching. In these chapters Luke also stresses how effective and remarkable Jesus' words were.

Second Part: The Ministry during the Ascent to Jerusalem

In this account of the long ascent of Jesus to Jerusalem, we find many of the teachings of Jesus which are proper to Luke and do not appear in either Matthew or Mark. These include the parables of the good Samaritan (Lk 10:25–37), mercy (Lk 15:1–32), the Pharisee and the publican (Lk 18:9–14), etc.

There is no clear unifying note, but Luke's characteristic features—prayer, mercy, the universality of salvation, riches and poverty, etc.—appear in these chapters.

Third Part: The Ministry in Jerusalem

This part, very similar to the parallel sections of Matthew and Mark, includes the entry into Jerusalem and the purification of the Temple (Lk 19:28–48), Jesus' controversies with the Jewish authorities (Lk 20:1–47), the eschatological discourse (Lk 21:5–36), the Passion (Lk 22:1–23, 56), and the Resurrection (Lk 24:1–53). Jesus is presented as a model of conduct for the Christian because of his mercy, greatness of soul, and recourse to prayer. The narrative ends as the book of Acts begins: with the command of our Lord to the apostles to remain in Jerusalem until the coming of the Holy Spirit and the Ascension.

4. Principal Contents of the Gospel

Jesus, Prophet, Savior, and Lord, a Model for Disciples

The most important thing about Luke, like the other Gospels, is what it teaches concerning Jesus Christ. He is presented as Prophet, Savior, and Lord. But that is not all. For the Evangelist, Jesus is the "new man," whose offspring, so to speak, are the disciples. For this reason, he is the head and model for Christians.

Prophet, Savior, and Lord. Jesus is called prophet in various places (Lk 7:16; 9:19; 13:33; 24:19). Since he is true God and true Man, he is the prophet *par excellence*: no one can speak in the name of God as he could (Lk 4:18, 43; 9:45; 19:21). Even in the Old Testament, prophets were moved by the Spirit of God; St. Luke underlines the profound and mysterious union of the *Holy Spirit* with the prophetic ministry of our Lord. Thus, at the baptism of Jesus, which marks the beginning of his public ministry, the Holy Spirit descends visibly upon him. Then the Spirit leads him into the desert where he is tempted, leads him into Galilee, etc. (Lk 3:22; 4:11, 14). Jesus takes on the prophetic vocation in the synagogue of Nazareth when he reads the text of Isaiah—"The Spirit of the Lord is upon me, because he has anointed me to preach good news to the poor." This, he affirms, is fulfilled in himself (cf. Lk 4:16–30).

The Gospel of St. Luke teaches throughout that Jesus Christ is the Savior of mankind. The narrative of the infancy highlights the fulfillment in Christ of the ancient promises of salvation made by God to the patriarchs and prophets of the chosen people: the child who has been born is the Savior awaited for so many centuries. Mary exults with joy in God her Savior (Lk 1:47); the angels, at the Nativity, announce that "today there is born to you, in the city of David, the Savior who is Christ, the Lord." (Lk 2:11). God had shown saving power (Lk 1:69) "to save us from our enemies (Lk 1:71). Salvation is announced by the Baptist so that the people will know that it entails the forgiveness of their sins (Lk 1:77). The eyes of Simeon see it when he recognizes the Child Jesus (Lk 2:30). All men see it, as Isaiah had prophesied (Lk 3:6). It comes to the sinful woman (Lk 7:50), to the Samaritan leper who returns to give thanks to Jesus (Lk 17:17), and Zachaeus attains it with the visit of the Master (Lk 19:9), etc. Salvation is also manifested in the cure of diseases, the pardon of sins, and reconciliation. Indeed, on many occasions St. Luke uses the verb "save" to signify a cure: the cure of the woman with a hemorrhage (Lk 8:43–48); of the blind man of Jericho (Lk 18:35–42); the raising of the daughter of Jairus (Lk 8:50); the freeing of the possessed Gerasene (Lk 8:26–39); etc.

Jesus is also the *Lord*. "Lord" is the word used to refer to God in order to avoid pronouncing his proper name, now usually written as Yahweh. It was also a term of respect for a person. St. Luke makes by far the greatest use of this title in his writing: 103 times in the Gospel and 107 in the Acts of the Apostles. Jesus is the Lord in the most profound sense from the moment of his birth, and was manifested as such in his resurrection. To him therefore is reserved the glory that will be especially manifested at the Second Coming. He is also the Lord of history.

Jesus, the "new man," model of a disciple. We saw earlier that Luke presents his work as a history of salvation reaching its culmination in Jesus Christ. In this history of salvation, as noted, the infancy narrative is something like a conclusion of the Old Testament and the opening of the New. From an Israel faithful to God, the chosen people, arises salvation for all nations. But St. Luke traces the divine plan even further, in the genealogy of Jesus going back to Adam who, he says, was "the son of God" (Lk 3:38). The parallelism, noted also in other places in the Gospel, is easy to establish: God created Adam from the mud of the earth through the vivifying action of the Holy Spirit; and he created the new man, Jesus Christ, through the descent of the Spirit upon the Blessed Virgin Mary, model of all those who are faithful to God.

To this St. Luke adds something else: what Jesus does is a model for what Christians are to do. This theme is present in the exhortations of Jesus in the Gospel and also in the Acts of the Apostles, where the first Christians are shown imitating their Master.

Jesus, then, is both new man and model for the disciple. Various traits present in Jesus should be imitated by his disciples.

1. Like Jesus, his disciple should be detached from *everything*, open to being wherever his mission leads him

(Lk 9:52–66). Many texts make this point: "Blessed are you poor, because yours is the Kingdom of God" (Lk 6:20); "And when Jesus heard it, he said to him, 'One thing you still lack. Sell all that you have and distribute to the poor, and you will have treasure in heaven; and come, follow me'" (Lk 18:22); "And when they had brought their boats to land, they left everything and followed him" (Lk 5:11), etc.

2. This detachment is the root of interior *freedom* in *joy*. Luke has an abundance of terms to signify joy: happiness, rejoicing, praise, etc. "And you will have joy and gladness, and many will rejoice at his birth" (Lk 1:14); "And entering, he said, 'Hail, full of grace, the Lord is with you!'" (Lk 1:28); "Rejoice in that day, and leap for joy, for behold, your reward is great in heaven" (Lk 6:23); "Just so, I tell you, there will be more joy in heaven over one sinner who repents than over ninety-nine righteous persons who need no repentance" (Lk 15:7).

3. The new man is a man of constant *prayer*, above all in the face of trial; just as Jesus prayed at his baptism, before the choice of the apostles, at the Transfiguration, in Gethsemane, and on the Cross.

4. The disciple becomes part of a new community, which Jesus guides and to which he transmits his salvific power, as we see above all in Acts. Assisted by this power and docile to the Holy Spirit, the disciple will give fruit, even when that is beyond human expectation.

5. Mercy is another characteristic of the disciple and has a central place in Christian life. God is full of mercy (Lk 1:72); the Father forgives and pardons (cf. Lk 15); Christ manifests mercy in being moved by others' needs (Lk 11:13; 15:2); he asks it of all mankind (Lk 10:39). As in Matthew the central exhortation of the Sermon on

the Mount is "Be perfect as your heavenly Father is perfect," so in Luke it is "*Be merciful, even as your Father is merciful*" (Lk 6:36). The Christian should imitate God, and Jesus Christ is the model.

6. This model of life must also be considered from the point of view of the disciple. Who can be a disciple of Christ? Who truly turns to God and follows Christ? The parable of the sower speaks of different ways of receiving the Word. Some fail to resist temptation; others are suffocated by the "concerns, riches, and pleasures of life"; but there also are those who "hearing the word, hold it fast in an honest and good heart, and bring forth fruit with patience" (Lk 8:15). The Greek words translated here as "honest and good heart" are *kale kai agathe*. These terms refer to the ideal of Greek manhood, the gentleman, the man of virtue, who is as he should be (Plato, Theaetetus). The virtuous man receives the seed of the Gospel gladly and bears fruit. Curiously, just after this passage, St. Luke introduces the episode in which Jesus says, "My mother and my brothers are those who hear the word of God and fulfill it" (Lk 8:21). This implies that the primary model for following Christ is his mother. We shall return to this later.

Here, then, is the context for the "following" of Christ by mercy, detachment, prayer, etc. The Gospel of St. Luke emphasizes, however, that these virtues and attitudes must be lived out here and now. The life of the Christian follows Jesus' path in his long ascent to Jerusalem culminating in the Cross and his glorification. The first thing one must do to imitate the Master is bear the Cross *every day*. "And he said to all, 'If any man would come after me, let him deny himself and take up his cross daily and follow me'" (Lk 9:23).

The Universality of Salvation

St. Luke's two books underline the fact that the goods announced by the prophets are fulfilled in Christ and in his Church, where he continues to live. These goods are offered not only to the Jews but to all peoples.

The universality of the salvation accomplished by Jesus Christ is depicted at length in the Acts of the Apostles, but it is already present in Luke's Gospel, both implicitly and explicitly. The Canticle of Simeon proclaims that salvation has been prepared "in the presence of all peoples" and that Jesus is "a light for revelation to the Gentiles" (Lk 2:29–32). Like the other synoptic Evangelists, St. Luke also applies to the mission of John the Baptist the text of Isaiah 40, but he extends the citation by one additional verse, namely that which declares ". . . and all flesh shall see the salvation of God" (Is 40:5; Lk 3:6). In the synagogue of Nazareth Jesus announces the future outreach to non-Jews; and later he explains to his disciples that his suffering and rising have been prophesized, and in his name conversion and forgiveness of sins was to be preached to all nations (Lk 24:47). Among all the texts, the most notable may be the one that speaks of Jesus' acceptance of the Samaritans, a people who then were enemies of the Jews. St. Luke does not include the injunction of Matthew 10:5 regarding the Samaritans—"Do not go to the land of the Gentiles, nor enter a city of the Samaritans"—which seemed to limit the disciples' mission to the territory of the Jews. But Jesus is shown rebuking his disciples who asked that the Samaritans be punished (Lk 9:55); he offers as an example of a true neighbor the good Samaritan (Lk 10:25-37); and, of the ten Lepers cured by Jesus, the one who returns to thank him is a Samaritan (Lk 17:16).

The Blessed Virgin Mary

The third Gospel presents the Mother of Christ in a special light, revealing with exquisite delicacy the greatness and beauty of the soul of the Blessed Virgin. No one—outside Jesus himself—is described in the Gospel stories with as much love and admiration as the Virgin Mary. This may explain the tradition that St. Luke painted Mary's portrait (but the claim is first made rather late, in the sixth century, when Theodorus the Lector asserted that Luke painted a picture of our Lady, that was sent from Jerusalem to Constantinople).

It is clear from the Gospel that no other human being has received such high and singular graces as Mary: she is "full of grace"; the Lord is with her; she has found favor before God; she has conceived by the action and grace of the Holy Spirit, becoming the Mother of Jesus without ceasing to be a virgin. Intimately united to the redemptive mystery of the Cross, she is to be blessed by all generations, inasmuch as the all-powerful One has done great things in her. With reason, a woman of the people praises the Mother of Jesus with enthusiasm and in a most expressive way (Lk 11:27).

Our Lady corresponded to such great divine gifts with the most generous fidelity. She receives with humility the announcement of the archangel regarding her dignity as Mother of God. She asks with simplicity what she should do to please God in everything. She commits herself fully to the divine plans. She is joyfully thankful for the gifts she has received, and faithfully observes the laws of God and the pious customs of her people. St. Elizabeth called her blessed because she believed. She is pained by the loss of her Child and complains to him, yet calmly accepts what at that time she is not able to understand. Mary knows how to contemplate with admiration the divine mysteries that she keeps and reflects on in her heart.

The inspired author of the third Gospel provides many signs pointing us to the realization that Mary is the personification of perfect human correspondence to God's will. Let us consider two aspects of this:

- A disciple is one who, with a good and generous heart, hears the word of God and keeps it. St. Luke shows Mary being proclaimed as the one who does this. Similar in its import is the statement—repeated twice—that "Mary kept all these things, pondering them in her heart" (Lk 2:19; cf. 2:51). Mary thus appears as the perfect model of the disciple of Christ. Moreover, she is exemplary for her following the path of Christ, as pointed out, for example, in the prophecy of Simeon.

- **A final point.** The Beatitudes, as given by St. Matthew, seem to be directed to all men: Blessed is the one who is poor, meek, etc. In St. Luke, however, they seem directed to Christians: Blessed are you who are now poor, who suffer, etc. It is noteworthy that when St. Luke uses this formula elsewhere, the reference is either explicitly to the Blessed Virgin (Lk 1:45, 48; 11:27, 28) or it could include her. Clearly, then, St. Luke wants us to see Mary as an example for Christ's disciples. And when the Holy Spirit descends on the apostolic group to launch the activity of the Church, the disciples are united around the Mother of Jesus (Acts 1:14).

7

The Gospel According to St. John

Juan Chapa

The Gospel of St. John is the last of the Gospels accepted by the Church as sacred and canonical. Like the synoptics, it announces the Good News; but, by comparison with the others, it presupposes a deeper understanding of the life and teaching of our Lord. It makes particularly clear the pre-existence of Christ. Jesus is the *Logos* of God who became man and, through his words and the signs that he works, reveals the Father. Faith in Jesus involves knowing the Father, having communion with him and with the Son, and living this communion by fulfilling his commandments.

Mark presents Jesus as Servant of God, Matthew as the Jewish Messiah, Luke as Lord and Savior; but John reveals Jesus as Son of God, eternal and pre-existent, who became man to reveal the Father and bring us to eternal life through his death and his resurrection. This profound understanding of the mystery of Christ is why the Gospel of John has come definitively to occupy its place as a continuation of the synoptics, although in some ancient Western codices one finds it after the Gospel of St. Matthew.

1. AUTHOR, DATE, AND PLACE OF COMPOSITION

Like the other Gospels, that of St. John does not give its author's name. Unlike the synoptics, however, the fourth Gospel identifies its author as someone present at scenes it narrates, in particular a disciple especially loved by Jesus. The conclusion of the Gospel explicitly says: "This is the disciple who is bearing witness to these things, and who has written these things; and we know that his testimony is true" (Jn 21:24). This refers to the disciple mentioned in verse 20 of the same chapter, "the disciple whom Jesus loved, who had lain close to his breast at the supper and had said, 'Lord, who is it that is going to betray you?'" and of whom it was rumored that "he would not die" (Jn 21:23). He is the same one mentioned at the foot of the cross (Jn 19:26), who ran with Peter to see the vacant tomb (Jn 20:2). Undoubtedly he was one of the closest disciples, for he was there when the risen Lord appeared to them on the shores of the Lake of Tiberius (Jn 21:7 ff).

In this beloved disciple of Jesus, the Tradition of the Church has recognized from very early on the apostle John, son of Zebedee. The first to affirm this is St. Irenaeus: "John, the disciple of the Lord, the same who reposed upon his breast, published the Gospel during his stay in Ephesus" (*Contra Haereses*, 3,1,1). St. Irenaeus was the Bishop of Lyons, but he was born around the year 130 in Smyrna (Asia Minor), where he knew St. Polycarp. His testimony has great value since, according to Tertullian,[1] St. Polycarp was instituted as bishop of Smyrna by St. John himself.

The *Canon of Muratori*, written in Rome about the year 180, has a prologue against Marcion and his followers, saying in part: "The Gospel of John was communicated and manifested to the churches by John himself, while he was still alive, according to what Papias of Hierapolis said." It also says:

> The fourth Gospel is by John, one of the disciples. When
> his co-disciples and bishops encouraged him, John said:

---

1. Tertullian, *Contra Omnes Haereses*, 32.

"Fast with me for three days starting today and whatever is revealed to us let us tell each other." That same night it was revealed to Andrew, one of the apostles, that John should write everything in his own name and that they should review it.

Eusebius in his *Historia Ecclesiastica* also refers to the testimony of Clement of Alexandria, who passed on a tradition according to which John composed his Gospel after the other Evangelists wrote theirs.

The three Gospels that were written earlier having been published, they also reached his hands, they say he accepted them and also gave testimony as to their truthfulness, but that the account lacked the things that Christ carried out in the beginning and also in the beginning of his preaching (*Historia Ecclesiastica*, 3,24,7).

Eusebius also has another citation from Clement. After referring to the authority of the synoptics, he reports, Clement said:

But the last of all, John, knowing that the external works (*ta somatika*) had already been shown clearly in the Gospels, urged by his friends and inspired by the Holy Spirit, composed a spiritual Gospel (*pneumatikon*). (*Historia Ecclesiastica*, 6,14,507)

From the fourth century it is the common and constant tradition to attribute the fourth Gospel to the apostle St. John.

A few authors, nevertheless, hold that Irenaeus was confused in referring to John the apostle as the author of the Gospel. Instead, they say, the author was John the Presbyter, a disciple of Jesus mentioned by Papias of Hierapolis, who lived in the first half of the second century and knew St. John. Eusebius cites the following text of Papias:

And if some time there come someone who had followed the ancients, I observe the words of the ancients, that is what was said by Andrew, or Peter, or Philip, or James, or John, or Matthew, or by any of the other disciples of the Lord, and including what was said by Aristion and the priest [or elder] John, disciples of the Lord, because I believe that one cannot get the same profit from what one learns in books as from what one learns by means of a living and lasting voice. (*Historia Ecclesiastica*, 3,39,5)

Although Papias certainly refers to two different people named John, at no time does he say who was author of the fourth Gospel. In contrast, Eusebius, clarifying the citation of Papias, explains that the first John mentioned is the apostle and Evangelist.

It is worthwhile indicating that [Papias] mentions the name of John twice. The first is on the list of Peter, James, Matthew, and the other apostles, clearly referring to the Evangelist; the second, once the discourse is concluded, he puts together with others, separate from the apostles and preceded by Aristion, calling him more clearly an elder. (*Historia Ecclesiastica*, 3,39,5)

The internal testimony of the Gospel and comparison with the synoptics support the identification of John the son of Zebedee as the beloved disciple: on the one hand, it would be difficult to explain the anonymity of this disciple in the fourth Gospel except on the supposition that he is the Gospel's author; on the other hand, literary features indicate that the testimony of the text is that of someone close to Jesus. The style has a clear Semitic feel to it, and the author knows the geography of Palestine and the Jewish world well. Other proposals that have been made concerning the identity of the beloved disciple raise greater difficulties than the traditional identification with John the apostle.

The Date of Composition

Testimonies from the beginning of the second century citing phrases from the Gospel or alluding to certain expressions, and papyri bearing fragments of the fourth Gospel found in Egypt, show the great authority it enjoyed and establish a date before which it must have been written.

1. Among the first references to the Gospel of St. John are those of St. Ignatius of Antioch (d. 107–115). He speaks of the Spirit who knows whence he comes and where he goes,[2] and says that the Word, the Son of God, was pleasing in all things to the one who sent him.[3] St. Polycarp, in his letter to the Philadelphians (c. 110), also evokes phrases in the Gospel of John. So does St. Justin (c. 150) in saying it is necessary to be born again to enter into the Kingdom of Heaven.[4] These dates indicate that the Gospel could not have been composed much later than the year 100.

2. The oldest fragment from the papyri of Egypt is the one known as P22. It was found in El-Fayum (Middle Egypt) and is preserved in the John Rylands library in Manchester. Dating from the first half of the second century, it is the oldest extant New Testament text. This and two other papyri show that around the year 200 the fourth Gospel was well known in the Nile country; very probably it was already being read in Upper Egypt in the first half of the second century. A book which had spread as far as Upper Egypt and whose authority was recognized around the year 150 must have been written considerably earlier, probably toward the end of the first century A.D. or very close to the beginning of the second century.

---

2. Cf. Jn 1:11; 7:28; 8:29.

3. Cf. Jn 3:5.

4. Cf. Jn 3:5.

3. On the other hand, certain expressions, the literary style, an apparent knowledge of Luke's Gospel—usually thought to date from the decade of the seventies—and the view taken of the words and deeds of Jesus suggest that this Gospel cannot have been too much earlier.

The traditional and most commonly accepted view is that the fourth Gospel was written between the years 90 and 100. The following considerations support this.

1. It seems likely that the Gospel of John reflects a situation in which the Christians have definitively separated from Judaism and been expelled from the synagogues. These developments can be traced to Judaism's new configuration after the first Jewish war (66–70 A.D.). With the Romans' destruction of the Temple in the year 70, and thanks to the activity of the Yamnia Academy (also called Yabneh, near today's Tel-Aviv) at the end of the first century, the Pharisee line was reconstituted and became dominant, giving rise to rabbinic Judaism. The Jewish communities spread through the cities of the Empire followed this new strain of Judaism. The leaders rejected whatever did not fit in with their thinking and expelled from the synagogues whoever deviated from their traditions, including Judeo-Christians.

2. This tension between Judaism and Christianity is obvious in the Gospel of St. John. For Judaism, John uses "the Jews"—an expression that appears some sixty times in the Gospel and corresponds to the usage of a pagan society in which Jews were a recognizable group, with the Pharisees as their leaders. The Judaism of John's Gospel appears to be the new line of reconstituted Phariseeism. Within this historical framework, some take references to "exclusion from the synagogue" for confessing Jesus as Christ—an expression found only in

John[5]—as a reflection of something added by the Yamnia Academy to the prayer of the 18 blessings (*Shemoneh Esreh*): "There is no hope for apostates . . . / . . . May the Nazarenes and the *minim* (sectarians) perish in an instant . . . / . . . Blessed are you, Lord, who subjects the tyrants." "Nazarenes" is the term for Christians.

3. The Jewish feasts are presented in the fourth Gospel as the framework within which Jesus acts to establish a new salvific economy. This indicates that the community to which the Gospel is directed sees itself apart from the old Jewish institutions as the true and new Israel. The new religion is understood to be a substitute for Judaism.

Since this confrontation with Judaism took shape at the end of the first century, it is logical to think that, as Tradition also agrees, the Gospel was composed in the decade of the nineties. Still, there is no lack of authors who argue for a date earlier than 70 or well into the second century.

1. Those who hold that the Gospel was written before the year 70 tend to fix upon aspects in it that are very Jewish. For example, John uses the words "rabbi" and "messiah" more often than the other Gospels; and the Temple, which was destroyed in the year 70, receives more attention in John than in the other books of the New Testament, suggesting that it was still standing when John was written. The fourth Gospel emphasizes more than the others Jesus' superiority in relation to John the Baptist—a preoccupation corresponding to an early stage. Finally, John appears frequently to use the

---

5. Jn 9:22: "His parents said this because they feared the Jews, for the Jews had already agreed that if any one should confess him to be Christ, he was to be put out of the synagogue." 12:24: "Nevertheless many even of the authorities believed in him, but for fear of the Pharisees they did not confess it, lest they should be put out of the synagogue." Cf. 16:2: "They will put you out of the synagogues; indeed, the hour is coming when whoever kills you will think he is offering service to God."

language of the manuscripts of Qumran, a community that ceased to exist in the year 70. But despite these considerations, the majority of exegetes do not accept the dating of the Gospel before 70.

2. Those who believe it was written in the second century cite an alleged lack of explicit testimonies among early Christian authors. They maintain that the earliest are from the end of the second century, roughly the years 160–170, while denying that authors like Ignatius and Justin knew the fourth Gospel. The other principal reason is that the Gospel's theology is in their judgment too sophisticated for a very early period and had to be the fruit of a slow evolution in the Church. Due to the discovery of the papyri from the beginning of the second century, however, few today still defend a very late date for this Gospel.

Thus there appear to be no serious objections to holding that the fourth Gospel was written no later than the end of the first century.

The Place of Composition

The common tradition of the Church affirms that from Jerusalem John moved to Ephesus. From there he was exiled to the island of Patmos, on the coast of Asia Minor. But later he returned to Ephesus, where he lived to an old age in the times of Trajan (years 98–117) and died a natural death. Testimony is given to this by Irenaeus (*Contra Haereses*, 2,22,3; 3,1,2), Justin (*Dialogue with Tryphon*, 81,4), and Clement of Alexandria (*Is There Salvation for the Rich?* 42). Eusebius of Caesarea alludes to them while adding the testimony of Apollonius and Policrates (*Historia Ecclesiastica*, 3,23,3–4; 3,39,3–4; 4,18,6–8; 5,8,4; 5,18,14; 5,20,6). The apocryphal *Acts of John*, from the middle of the second century, also says John lived in Ephesus. Tertullian, for his part, says John died very old (*A Treatise on the Soul*, 50). These considerations point to Ephesus as the place where the Gospel was written.

2. LITERARY AND THEOLOGICAL CHARACTERISTICS

Language and Style

The fourth Gospel is written in a rather simple Greek *koine*, similar to that spoken in the Mediterranean world by persons who were not native Greek speakers. From the literary point of view it is not especially rich. Its 15,635 words are drawn from a total vocabulary of only 1,011 words. The longest sentence is Jn 13:1: "Now before the feast of the Passover, when Jesus knew that his hour had come to depart out of this world to the Father, having loved his own who were in the world, he loved them to the end." The shortest is that of Jn 11:35: "Jesus wept," which is also the shortest verse of the whole Bible.

The style is direct, the syntax rather elementary, with short sentences and phrases tending to follow one another without any connecting words. Nevertheless it possesses the strength of a mature work, with great literary intensity that centers on the figure of Jesus.

The vocabulary, though limited, is unified. There is no difference between that of the narrator and that of the persons who appear in the Gospel. Prominent include: *aletheia, alethes, alethinos* (truth, the true), *ginoskein* (to know), *zoe* (life), *ioudaioi* (the Jews), *kosmos* (the world), *martyrein, martyria* (to bear witness, testimony), *pater* (referring to God), *pemein* (to send, to be sent), *terein* (to guard), *phaneroun* (to manifest), *phos* (light). There is a notable absence of terms favored by the synoptics: *euaggelion* (gospel), *dynamis* (power), *kalein* (to call), *katharein* (purify, clean), *keryssein* (proclaim), *metanoia* (conversion), *parabole* (parable).

Some see in the Gospel's language and ideas a dependence on various cultural and religious surroundings. So John is said to be strongly influenced by works of the Jewish Hellenistic world (Philo), while others link him to Qumran or see a connection with Gnostic circles. Yet the fourth Gospel is strongly rooted in the Old Testament tradition; and there are no solid reasons for claiming that John depends on extra-biblical influences, although some vocabulary and some ideas may be shared. The style manifest the author's Semitic background: he is, as has been said, quite familiar with the geography of Palestine and the customs and feasts of the Jewish world.

Composition and Publication

On reading the fourth Gospel, certain details are at once apparent that seem to break the thread of the narrative and lead one to suspect that the writing took place in several stages. Most significant are the following:

1. **The order of chapters 4–5–6.** The activity of Jesus in Jerusalem described in chapter 5 on the occasion of an unspecified feast does not seem consistent with his presence in Galilee in chapters 4 and 6. The final verse of chapter 4 says, "This was now the second sign that Jesus did when he had come from Judea to Galilee." Chapter 5 begins, "After this there was a feast of the Jews, and Jesus went up to Jerusalem," and the whole of chapter 5 takes place there. Chapter 6 then begins as follows: "After this Jesus went to the other side of the Sea of Galilee, which is the Sea of Tiberias." Some hold that chapter 5 was a later addition placed between chapters 4 and 6, or that it belongs in the context of chapter 7.

2. **The connection of chapters 14–15.** In chapter 15, there is a brusqueness to the resumption of Jesus' discourse at the Last Supper. After the conclusion of chapter 14

("Rise, let us go hence"), it seems rather surprising to find: "I am the true vine, and my Father is the vinedresser" (Jn 15:1). "Rise, let us go hence" seems a better lead-in to the beginning of chapter 18: "When Jesus had spoken these words, he went forth with his disciples across the Kidron valley, where there was a garden, which he and his disciples entered."

3. **Appendix (chapter 21).** The account of Jesus' appearance on the shores of the lake in chapter 21 is a later addition. It speaks of the beloved disciple, the author of this testimony, as someone who was presumably dead by then ("The saying spread abroad among the brethren that this disciple was not to die; yet Jesus did not say to him that he was not to die, but, 'If it is my will that he remain until I come, what is that to you?'" Jn 21:23). It then concludes with words similar to those at the end of the previous chapter: "Now Jesus did many other signs in the presence of the disciples, which are not written in this book; but these are written that you may believe that Jesus is the Christ, the Son of God, and that believing you may have life in his name" (Jn 20:30–31). Although this would seem to be an appropriate finish, chapter 21 then tells of the appearance at the Lake of Tiberias and provides another ending: "This is the disciple who is bearing witness to these things, and who has written these things; and we know that his testimony is true. But there are also many other things which Jesus did; were every one of them to be written, I suppose that the world itself could not contain the books that would be written" (Jn 21:24–25).

These and other literary features seems to indicate that the Gospel's present form is the work of a final editor who redacted already existing material under the guidance of the Spirit, and supplied the order it now has. While declaring the community's conviction in saying "we know that his testimony is true," this final editor also points to "the disciple whom Jesus loved" as the one who "is bearing witness to these things, and who has written these things" (Jn 21:24; cf. 21:20).

Various hypotheses have been proposed regarding the process of composition of the Gospel and thereby to explain more profound aspects of Johanine Christology. Some have seen at work here the development of the community that formed around the beloved disciple and supposedly took on the character of the schools of antiquity, both Hellenistic (Pythagoras, Plato, Aristotle, Epicurus), and Jewish (Hillel, Shammai, Philo). A school was based upon its founder, an eminent thinker who gathered disciples about him. These then developed his doctrine and, at times, also followed his way of life. In the present instance, the "school" would originate with the apostle John, son of Zebedee, who left Palestine for Ephesus, perhaps passing through Syrian Antioch. He and the disciples who followed him would have been the core of the Christian communities that John directed, scattered throughout the great cities of Asia Minor as one sees in the seven churches of the Book of Revelation.

Purpose of the Writing and Comparison with the Synoptics

The fourth Evangelist writes, as he himself says, "that you may believe that Jesus is the Christ, the Son of God, and that believing you may have life in his name" (Jn 20:31). He aims to form and strengthen his readers' faith. To that end he follows a plan different from that of the synoptics.

1. **The geographic and chronological framework.** John focuses above all on the activity of Jesus in Judea and in the Temple of Jerusalem, where our Lord goes at least three times at the time of feasts (Jn 2:13; 7:10; 12:12); he gives only a few details of Jesus' activity in Galilee. The

passage through Samaria (Jn 4:1–42) also is emphasized. Reference to Jesus' presence in Jerusalem for three Passover feasts implies that his ministry lasted at least three years. In contrast, the first three Evangelists tell of only one trip to the Holy City during his public ministry— that in which he died during the feast of the Pasch. In their account, the ministry of Jesus seems to have lasted just one year.

2. **Miracles.** Of the twenty-nine miracles described by the synoptics, St. John refers to only two (the multiplication of the loaves and Jesus' walking on the water);[6] however, he speaks of five other miracles (at the marriage feast of Cana, the cure of the son of the royal official, the cure of the paralytic at the Probatic pool, the cure of the man born blind in Jerusalem, and the raising of Lazarus).[7] The most notable feature of his account, however, is that he present these miracles as "signs" that point to express realities more profound than appears on the surface. With the marriage feast of Cana, the first of the signs, the glory of Jesus is manifested, the beginning of the Messianic era is revealed, and one can already see the role of his mother, the Blessed Virgin Mary, in the redemption (Jn 2:1–11); the multiplication of the loaves and fishes, recounted also by the synoptics, provides support for the words of Christ when he presents himself as the Bread of Life; the cure of the man born blind precedes the manifestation of Jesus as light of the world (ch. 9); the raising of Lazarus teaches that Jesus alone is the Resurrection and the Life (ch. 11).

3. **The Passion of Jesus.** In his account of the Passion, death, and resurrection of Jesus, the fourth Evangelist agrees

---

6. Jn 6:11, 19.
7. Jn 2:1–11; 4:46–54; 5:1–9; 9:1–41; 11, 33–44.

with the synoptics but tells of these events from a different perspective—that of the glorification of Christ: "the hour" of Jesus is manifested (Jn 2:4; 7:30; 13:1; 17:1) and the Father glorifies the Son, who in dying conquers the devil, sin, and death and is exalted over all things (Jn 12:32–33). When recounting Jesus' predictions of his Passion, the synoptics stress the appropriateness of the suffering of the Son of Man (Mt 16:21 and parallel passages), while St. John emphasizes the appropriateness of his *being exalted* (Jn 3:14–15; 8:28; 12:32–33).

4. **Teaching.** The fourth Evangelist also treats Jesus' teachings in his own special manner. For example, he refers only twice to "the Kingdom of Heaven" (both times, in the dialogue with Nicodemus, Jn 3:3, 5), while the synoptics mention it much more often.[8] St. John does not deal with a number of subjects found in the three first Gospels, such as the question of the Sabbath, pharisaical legalism, etc.; while in contrast he speaks of life, truth, light, glory—subjects that hardly appear in the synoptics. John also presents the preaching of Jesus in long discourses that contrast in certain ways with the other three Gospels. The latter employ many images and parables drawn from everyday things and popular customs, and expressed in direct language; John's language is frequently metaphorical or symbolic (light, truth, water, spirit, the testimony of God, etc.), and makes use of significant formulae ("I am," "you in me and I in you," "remain in me," etc.). He likes antitheses (light-darkness, life-death, being from here below-being from there above, truth-falsehood) and frequently uses expressions with a double meaning, simultaneously material and spiritual (exalt, see, look).

Still, the fourth Gospel has many points in common with the synoptics. It is a true Gospel. John writes, as he himself

---

8. Jn 3:5; cf. Mt 3:2; 4:23; 5:3; 11:12; 13:24, etc.

says, "that you may believe that Jesus is the Christ, the Son of God, and that believing you may have life in his name" (Jn 20:31): he writes, in other words, to strengthen and form the faith of his readers, and this statement is enough by itself to mark out the work as, generically, a Gospel. Like the other Gospels, it has its own characteristics: The emphasis on Jesus' identity as Messiah and his divine filiation, reflected in his miracles. John aims to foster faith in Christ, and the elements he uses to this end—Jesus' teachings and miracles—are fully part of the apostolic preaching, the proclamation of the *kerygma* (teaching) about the person and work of Jesus.

John's differences from the synoptics can be explained by his distinct perspective. At the conclusion of the Gospel, the author speaks of his intention to testify to what he *saw* (Jn 19:35; 21:24). This is his intention throughout, so that rather than use words like "evangelize" or "preach," he favors "witness," "testify," and "teach." The object of his testimony is always Jesus Christ—so that, for instance, he presents the teaching of the Baptist as testimony to Christ (Jn 1:7, 19, 32, 34; 3:26; 5:33). Above all, he insists that the Father testified to having sent Jesus (Jn 5:37). He also speaks of Jesus' testimony about himself, in that he knew whence he came and where he was going (Jn 8:14), and testified about what he had seen (Jn 3:11). The Scriptures also give testimony about him (Jn 14:39), as the Holy Spirit, whom he would send, would do. Finally, our Lord says to the apostles: "and you also are witnesses, because you have been with me from the beginning" (Jn 15:27). Thus, the written Gospel is the "testimony" given and received by the Church (Jn 21:24).

Its character of testimony stands against those who argue that the fourth Gospel was not the work of an eyewitness and think John used other sources (Bultmann, for example, speaks of a source for the discourses, another source for the miracles, and another for the account of the Passion). Such proposals exist in the realm of hypothesis, and although they offer explanations of some obscure points, they present many difficulties. Hypothesis also is operative regarding the author's knowledge and use of the synoptic Gospels. Some hold that he did not know them completely; others think he had one or more available, especially Luke (although for others, Mark). However that may be, the fourth Gospel plainly presupposes a depth of knowledge of the synoptic teaching.

Levels of Comprehension

The Gospel of St. John is distinctive in another aspect, as Clement of Alexandria indicates in calling it a "spiritual" Gospel. The Evangelist often speaks of the deepest meaning of Jesus' words and deeds, thus earning the title "the theologian."

Sometimes John distinguishes the time of the Gospel narrative from post-Resurrection time. His point is that although the story of Jesus is accessible to anyone, believer or not, its deeper meaning is accessible only to one who, in the light of faith, believes in Jesus who died and rose again.

Typical of apocalyptic writings, John shows that not just any hearer can grasp the mysteries of the Kingdom but only the recipient of a special divine revelation. This can be seen especially in certain of the dialogues between Jesus and others. Usually Jesus begins with an enigmatic statement that arouses curiosity ("The wind blows where it will," "Lazarus is sleeping," "The Son of Man has to be raised"), thus leading to a discourse that explains a specific doctrinal point. Think of Nicodemus—new life; or the Samaritan woman—living water. Jesus speaks of realities deeper than at first appears: The wind that blows is the Holy Spirit; the living water is grace, the Spirit's gift. Indeed, even the disciples fully understood the Master's meaning only after the coming of the Holy Spirit. (Jn 14:26). The Evangelist makes this point on several occasions,[9] when the Master, seeing their inability to understand, consoles them with the promise of the Spirit of Truth, who will guide them to the fullness of truth (Jn 16:13).

Thus John recounts Jesus' teaching and actions on two levels. On the first level, Jesus' proclamation can be understood by his hearers in light of their own biblical-religious Jewish background, which allows them to recognize him as the one in whom God's promises are realized. The other level implies that the proclamation is only intelligible after Easter, when its hearers recognize Jesus as not only the Messiah promised by God but the way that leads to the mystery of God's love for mankind through the mystery of the Son. For example, the Baptist's confession: "This is the Son of God" (Jn 1:34) is not an anachronism in the context of the Old Testament familiar to his hearers, but its meaning is much richer for readers of the Gospel: Jesus is Son of God in the sense of "only Son," as the prologue says.

People sometimes speak of the symbolic character of the fourth Gospel. A symbol joins two entities: something immediately perceptible by the senses and something invisible for which the sensible entity stands. In John whole narrative passages are symbolic. Not that what is related did not happen but that it has meaning beyond the surface of the narrative. Sensible realities point to the deep meaning of Jesus' deeds. For example, the episode of the purification of the Temple has a symbolic character, since it concludes with the teaching relating to the New Temple, Jesus himself. The whole of the Gospel similarly has a symbolic character: Jesus of Nazareth is a "symbol" of the Resurrected one, the one who, as the Gospel teaches, is glorified with the Father and present in the believers.

---

9. Cf. Jn 2:17, 22; 12:16; 13:7; 16:14.

It is important not to remain on the first level, seeking to reconstruct historically an event of the past, nor to dwell exclusively on the second level, as though the first were without importance. This resembles the relationship between the Old Testament and the New. The New Testament is not a substitute for the Old, but illuminates it and completes it. The first supplies roots for the second. When the Evangelist directs the reader's attention to Jesus of Nazareth, he does not mean only a historical figure of the past but Jesus, the *Word* made flesh.

In St. John, as in the synoptics, we find generally the same framework as was employed by the apostles in their oral preaching: After being baptized in the Jordan by John the Baptist, Jesus begins his public ministry; he preaches and works miracles in Galilee and Jerusalem; his life on earth ends with his Passion and glorious resurrection (cf. Acts 10:38–41). Within that framework, however, John emphasizes the succession of Jewish feasts and Jesus' progressive manifestation as Messiah and Son of God.

3. Structure

The Gospel's classic structuring is that of a division into two main parts, with a prologue. The parts are usually designated by the names originally given them by the Anglican exegete Charles H. Dodd: "the book of signs" and "the book of the Passion" (or "book of Glory"). In greater detail, the sequence is as follows.

The Prologue

Jesus is exalted as the eternal Word of God, Creator of the world together with the Father, and as true Light, become incarnate to communicate to the world definitive and saving revelation for all mankind (Jn 1:1–18).

First Part: Manifestation of Jesus as the Messiah through His Signs and Words

This extends from the testimony of John the Baptist concerning Jesus, to the Paschal feast in which his death takes place. After an introduction, including the first testimony of the Baptist (Jn 1:19–34) and the calling of the first disciples (Jn 1:3–51), we are told of the first manifestations of Jesus as author of the new salvific economy and of the first receptions of faith (Jn 2:1–4, 54). The narrative takes in his ministry in Galilee, a first trip to Jerusalem for the feast of the Passover, and Jesus' return to Galilee via Samaria. Then Jesus shows his divinity (Jn 5:1–47) while again visiting Jerusalem on the occasion of a feast. Back in Galilee again, he manifests himself as the Bread of Life (Jn 6:1–71). In Jerusalem once more, during the feast of Tabernacles, he reveals himself as the Light of the world (Jn 7:1–10, 21). Next he confronts the Jews in Jerusalem at the feast of the Dedication, presenting himself as one with the Father (Jn 10:22–42). In Bethany near Jerusalem he raises Lazarus and reveals himself as the Life of the world (Jn 11:1–57). Finally, after his anointing by Mary in Bethany, Jesus is acclaimed as Messianic King in Jerusalem (Jn 12:1–50).

Second Part: Manifestation of Jesus as the Messiah, Son of God, in His Passion, Death, and Resurrection

Beginning with the Last Supper—occasion of a manifestation of his innermost being—(Jn 13:1–17:26), the Gospel talks of Jesus' Passion and death (Jn 18:1–19:42), then closes with the appearances of the risen Christ (Jn 20:1–21:25). These, along with the empty tomb, testify to the reality of the resurrection. The risen Jesus infuses the Holy Spirit into his apostles, empowering them to forgive sins, and establishes Peter as the guide of his Church.

One could also use the Jewish feasts to trace the framework for Jesus' ministry, while at the same time showing that his coming renders them obsolete. In that case the Gospel might be divided along the following lines.

Prologue (Jn 1:1–18): Jesus is the Word of God made flesh.

Inaugural week (Jn 1:19–2:11): calling of the first disciples and manifestation of Jesus as the Messiah; the sign (miracle) at the marriage feast of Cana.

The first Passover (Jn 2:12–4:54): Jesus purifies the Temple and, crossing Samaria, goes to Galilee, where he perform his second sign in Cana.

The Sabbath (Jn 5:1–47): Jess cures a sick person at the Probatic pool; he is the new Moses who changes the precept of Sabbath rest.

The Passover of the Bread of Life (Jn 6:1–71): the miracle of the multiplication of the loaves; Jesus is the Bread of Life who replaces the manna.

The feast of Tabernacles (Jn 7:1–10:21): Jesus is the font of living water and the light of the world, who replaces the feast's ceremonies of water and of light; he gives sight to the man born blind.

The feast of the Dedication of the Temple (Jn 10:22–11:54): Jesus is consecrated in place of the altar of the Temple; the raising of Lazarus.

The final Passover week (Jn 11:55–19:42): Jesus is glorified through his death and resurrection.

The week of appearances of the Risen Christ (Jn 20:1–29): Jesus infuses the Spirit into his disciples.

Final appendix (Jn 21:1–25): The appearance in Galilee: Peter and the Church.

Many other ways of understanding this Gospel's structure have been suggested: chronological-geographical; liturgical;

psychological-dramatic, focused on the blindness of Judaism and culminating in the drama of the Passion; thematic, based on theological ideas; cyclical, emphasizing the same ideas worked out in different ways; symbolic, with the connecting thread the Exodus (the second Covenant follows the same path as the first), or even Genesis (the first creation is followed by a second, supernatural one realized in Christ); or numerical, based on the number seven. All these hypotheses about structure have advantages and disadvantages. None is fully satisfactory.

4. Principal Contents

The fourth Gospel presents the revelation of Jesus about the Father. The appropriate responses are shown to be faith and love. Faith and love unite Christ's disciples in the Church, where Christ lives and becomes present through the gifts of salvation, the sacraments. In addition Jesus has given his Mother, the Virgin Mary, to the Church, and she is also our Mother.

The Revelation of God

From a doctrinal and religious point of view, the crucial point about the fourth Gospel is that it shows how the invisible God made himself known through Jesus Christ: "No one has ever seen God; the only Son, who is in the bosom of the Father, he has made him known" (Jn 1:18). Only Jesus could have revealed God's inner nature, since he is the Word of God, the eternal Son, who truly knows the Father, and since, through his intercession and in his name, God sent his Spirit who made known the fullness of truth.

The Father. The starting point of everything is the Father and his will to love. From this will came all of creation and the desire for mankind's salvation (Jn 3:16), carried out through the mission of Jesus (Jn 3:17; 12:47). The Father sent Jesus to give him glory through revelation of his name and bring salvation to mankind.

Jesus Christ. Already in the prologue it is said that Jesus is the Word who was God; and at the same time he is declared to be consubstantial with the Father—from the beginning he was with God. Jesus is the only-begotten Son of the Father, not only united to the Father but having the same nature as the Father: "I and the Father are one" (Jn 10:30). He teaches that God is his Father in a manner different from the way men teach: "I am ascending to my Father and your Father" (Jn 20:17). Along with this fundamental reality, John presents the figure of Jesus with certain features of his own.

1. He is the *Logos* (the Word). This term had broad resonance in the Hellenistic world, but above all it draws upon the Wisdom Tradition of the Old Testament about the Wisdom of God personified acting in the world. John announces astonishing news: the *Logos* has become flesh (Jn 1:14).

2. He is the one sent by the Father to the world to save mankind and also is the Messiah, the King of salvation.

3. He is the Son of Man, who descends to earth to judge the world and returns to the Father. His ascent to heaven is an exaltation-glorification. Jesus comes from the Father and must return to him.

4. He is the Prophet, similar to Moses, promised in the Old Testament (Deut 18:15, 18), who would come at the end of times to announce definitive salvation.

5. He is the Lamb of God, who takes away the sins of the world. The death of Jesus is in effect a propitiatory sacrifice for mankind.

The Spirit. Jesus speaks of the Spirit as he does of ↑
as a Person. At the Last Supper, and again after the Resurrection, Jesus tells his followers of the Spirit and his revelatory
action. He himself will ask the Father to give them another
Consoler, the Spirit of Truth; and the Father will heed that
prayer of Christ and will send the Paraclete, who proceeds
from the Father and receives from the Son what he will come
to announce.[10]

The work of Christ is joined to the Spirit's action. The
Spirit descends upon him at his baptism. He creates a new
condition in man, a new birth (Jn 3:5), through the water of
baptism. He instructs the disciples and makes them understand the works and words of Jesus as the one who reveals
the Father, bringing them to the full truth and glorifying him
(Jn 14:26; 16:13). The Spirit also brings about the liberation
of man through the apostolic ministry: "Receive the Holy
Spirit. If you forgive the sins of any, they are forgiven; if you
retain the sins of any, they are retained" (Jn 20:22–23).

The Knowledge of God: Faith and Love

Faith. To believe, according to the fourth Gospel, involves
knowing the truth about Christ. Faith includes both the act
of trusting self-commitment and the act of knowing. John
tells us that this knowledge comes through his testimony and
through the action of the Spirit of truth.

Faith also is a judgment: those who believe in this way
already participate, in some manner, in divine life: "He who
believes in the Son has eternal life" (Jn 3:36); others do not
believe and are therefore already being judged by God: "He
who does not believe is condemned already, because he has
not believed in the name of the only Son of God" (Jn 3:18).
Thus Jesus' coming is the occasion for a judgment: man must

---

10. Jn 14:16–17; 15:26; 16:13; 14:26; 16:13–15.

choose between accepting or rejecting the revelation Jesus brings; and in making this decision, man judges himself.

Thus, besides a judgment at the end of time after which salvation will follow (the Gospel also refers to this), John emphasizes the here and now of salvation, which becomes present when one believes in Jesus. He who believes in Jesus Christ possesses eternal life, that is, participates in God's own life communicated through union with Jesus, as branches are united to a vine (Jn 15:1–8). Communicating that life is the purpose of God's revelation: "For God so loved the world that he gave his only Son, that whoever believes in him should not perish but have eternal life" (Jn 3:16). That life is a guarantee of resurrection at the end of time: "This is the will of my Father, that every one who sees the Son and believes in him should have eternal life; and I will raise him up at the last day" (Jn 6:40).

Love. Eternal life consists in knowing the Father and the Son—"And this is eternal life, that they know thee the only true God, and Jesus Christ whom thou hast sent" (Jn 17:3)— and that knowledge is at the same time a participation in the love between them: "I made known to them thy name, and I will make it known, that the love with which thou hast loved me may be in them, and I in them" (Jn 17–26).

The faith that communicates eternal life to man is thus inseparably united to love, since it consists precisely in entering into the relationship of love between the Father and the Son: "As the Father has loved me, so have I loved you; abide in my love" (Jn 15:9). Hence it should also be manifested in fraternal love, Jesus' unique commandment in the Gospel, in which he proposes himself as a model.[11] God took the initiative in love;

---

11. Jn 15:9–12. In 1 John 3:23 the commandment of Jesus appears in other words, but it coincides with the formulations of the Gospel. "And this is his commandment, that we should believe in the name of his Son Jesus Christ and love one another, just as he has commanded us."

and he who takes the initiative is he who loves the most. Love's greatness can be measured by the value of the gift given, and God gave what for him was most valuable, most loved, his own Son. Jesus responded with a love shown in the faithful fulfillment of the Father's will. He gave us an example so that we who are his disciples should do as he did.

The Church

In the fourth Gospel the new faith in Jesus appears as a replacement for the Jewish faith. Its references to the feasts underline this. Jesus came to bring a new form of worship, worship "in spirit and in truth" (Jn 4:23), and the disciples of Jesus form a community distinct from Judaism. Although the term "Church" does not appear in the fourth Gospel, the author shows us that he is a member of the group formed by the disciples of Jesus: as, for example, when he uses the first person plural to testify concerning Christ—"we have seen his glory" (Jn 1:14)—or guarantee the truth of what the apostle transmits—"and we know that his testimony is true" (Jn 21:24). In addition, in the Gospel Jesus' words are recalled describing those who believe in him as a sheepfold whose door is Christ himself, as well as those others in which, alluding to the Old Testament prophecies about the renewal of the people of Israel, Jesus presents himself as the Good Shepherd come to form a single flock of which all mankind should be part (Jn 10:11–17). That sheepfold and that flock refer to the Church. Similarly, the Church is symbolized by the vine to which branches are united (Jn 15:1–8). In this as in the previous images, Jesus Christ is shown as the one who rules and gives life to his Church, and he asks the Father that his disciples may enjoy the same unity that he and his Father do (Jn 17:21–23).

The role of Peter. The community that succeeded the disciples, the Church, is in continuity with the disciples who accompanied Jesus and gave testimony about him (Jn 20:31). Although the beloved disciple, whose testimony to Christ is found in the fourth Gospel (Jn 21:24), is prominent among them, chief among the disciples is Peter, first to enter the sepulchre and the one to whom the risen Christ gives the pastoring of the whole flock of believers (Jn 20:6–8; 21:15:19).

Signs and sacraments. Jesus' actions in the fourth Gospel can be said to have a sacramental character, for divine gifts are communicated in them by means of external signs. Jesus promises the disciples that they too will do such things; and after rising he gives them the Holy Spirit so that they can forgive sins, that is, enable people to be saved (Jn 14:12; 20:22–23). One enters the Church, the flock of Christ, by adhering to him by faith and by a new birth through water and the Spirit (Christian baptism, symbolized also in the account of the cure of the man born blind in John 3:8; 9:1–41). Christ's flock counts on being fed by the Bread of Life, the Flesh and the Blood of Christ, offered to believers in the Eucharist (Jn 6:48–59).

The Blessed Virgin Mary

A special feature of the fourth Gospel is the importance of certain women, including Martha and Mary, Mary Magdalene, and especially the Mother of our Lord, the Blessed Virgin. She appears twice, at the marriage feast of Cana and on Calvary. These are the beginning and the end of Jesus' manifestation as Messiah and Son of God, and indicate that Mary's presence takes in the whole of it. There is a clear parallelism between the two scenes: in both, our Lady is referred to as "the Mother of Jesus," and in both he calls her "woman." Moreover, both at Cana and on Calvary there is reference to Jesus' "hour," an hour that is his whole life.[12]

---

12. Cf. Jn 7:30; 8:20; 12:27; 13:1; 17:1.

Jesus' use of the word "woman" to speak to his Mother expresses solemnity and emphasis. Most commentators are inclined to see here an allusion to Genesis 3:15 which speaks of "the woman" and her line as victors over the serpent, symbol of the devil. The Fathers speak of a parallelism between Eve and Mary, similar to that between Adam and Christ (cf. Rom 5:12–14). In fact, in Christ's death we find the victory over the serpent, since in dying Christ redeemed us from slavery to the devil. *Mors per Evam, vita per Mariam,* death came to us through Eve, life through Mary.[13]

---

13. St. Jerome, *Letter to Eustochius*, 22, 21.

Some Examples

Juan Luis Caballero

Among the points made in this volume so far, four stand out.

1. It is necessary to read and study the Gospels in a way that challenges the rationalism which a priori rejects anything supernatural in Scripture.

2. Christian exegesis has shown how the faith professed by the Church in the truth of the Gospels is supported by historical data and reliable documents.

3. In doing so, Catholic exegesis has used the same scholarly tools, both literary and historical, used by rationalist scholarship: essentially the analysis of scriptural forms and the criteria of historicity.

4. The Gospels have been demonstrated to be a historically faithful rendering of events in the life of Jesus, the preaching of the apostles, and the teaching of the Evangelists.

Now, using examples, we shall see how this work of research has been carried out and its relevance for a non-specialist reader interested in learning to read the Gospels with greater understanding. In doing so, the principal steps of the process will be noted, with what is probable distinguished from what is certain.

1. THE CALLING OF MATTHEW AND THE MEAL WITH THE PUBLICAN

This episode, common to the three synoptic Gospels, serves our purpose well.

Mt 9:9–13	Mk 2:14–17	Lk 5:27–32
9 As Jesus passed on from there, he saw a man called *Matthew* sitting at the tax office; and he said to him,	14 And as he passed on, he saw Levi *the son of Alphaeus* sitting at the tax office, and he said to him,	27 After this he went out, and saw a tax collector, named *Levi*, sitting at the tax office; and he said to him,
"Follow me." And he rose and followed him.	"Follow me." And he rose and followed him.	"Follow me." 28 And *he left everything*, and rose and followed him.
10 And as he sat at table in the house, behold, many tax collectors and sinners came and sat down with Jesus and his disciples.	15 And as he sat at table in his house, many tax collectors and sinners were sitting with Jesus and his disciples; *for there were many who followed him.*	29 And *Levi* made him a great feast *in his house*; and there was a large company of tax collectors and others sitting at table with them.
11 And when the Pharisees saw this, they said to his disciples,	16 And the scribes of the Pharisees, when they saw that he was eating with sinners and tax collectors, said to his disciples,	30 And the Pharisees and their scribes murmured against his disciples, saying,
"Why does *your teacher* eat with tax collectors and sinners?"	"Why does he eat with tax collectors and sinners?"	"Why do you *eat and drink* with tax collectors and sinners?"

cont'd.

Mt 9:9–13 cont'd.	Mk 2:14–17 cont'd.	Lk 5:27–32 cont'd.
12 But when he heard it, he said, "Those who are well have no need of a physician, but those who are sick.	17 And when Jesus heard it, he said to them, "Those who are well have no need of a physi-cian, but those who are sick;	31 And Jesus answered them, "Those who are *well* have no need of a physician, but those who are sick;
13 *Go and learn what this means, 'I desire mercy, and not sacrifice.'* For I came not to call the righteous, but sinners."	I came not to call the righteous, but sinners."	32 I have not come to call the righteous, but sinners *to repentance.*"

Two things are described here: the call of Matthew (Levi) and the meal of Jesus with publicans and sinners that followed. These are two distinct actions: the call of a disciple—an account of a vocation—and Jesus' recurring behavior of receiving sinners and eating with them (cf. Lk 15:2). Let us begin by looking at the passages from the point of view of form criticism.

Analysis of Forms

The first account, one verse in Mark and Matthew and two in Luke, concerns a vocation. The structure is repeated many times in the Gospels—in the calls of Peter, Andrew, James, and John, the rich young man, the disciples who want to follow Jesus (Lk 9:52–66), etc. The schema, very stylized, is always much the same: Jesus meets someone, looks at him, and calls him to become his follower; the one called leaves what he is doing and follows Jesus. In the Gospel of St. John we see that there was probably some prior contact between

Jesus and those he chose as disciples, that this relationship tended to be favorable to following him, etc. Thus the passage under consideration here presents the essence of discipleship as lived in the time of Jesus and since then repeated in the Church: (1) a meeting with Christ, (2) a call to follow him, (3) an immediate response, leaving behind what one is doing, (4) thus implying that to follow him is to learn from him in order to imitate him.

The other event in this passage is the meal. It is often said to be what Dibelius calls a *paradigm* and Bultmann, an *apothegm*. This form appears similar to a common form in Hellenism, where it is called *chreia*—the sayings of teachers. The account is brief and simple, religiously colored by a teaching purpose focused on the final words of Jesus. Other examples of *paradigms* or *apothegms* are the controversy over the wheat plucked on the Sabbath (Mk 2:23–28), Martha and Mary (Lk 10:38–42), the blessing of the children (Mk 10:13 ff), etc.

In general, there is no doubt concerning the historicity of narratives like those describing the calling of various disciples. Yet in analyzing this section, Bultmann held that the two episodes had been linked by the Evangelist and there was no reason to keep them linked. His fundamental rationale for separating them is simply that he supposes the forms function independently. That the two episodes are related appears plausible, however; and a historical circumstance points to a personal recollection underlying the text. Excavations in Capernaum have found that the synagogue was at one end of the village and the lake at the other. Jesus is said to have left the synagogue and gone "once again to the shore of the lake. And the whole crowd went towards him and he taught them. As he passed by, he saw Levi . . ." (Mt 3:13). The evidence may not be conclusive, but it helps provide a basis for believing what the Gospel says. An exhaustive analysis would require comparing these accounts with other accounts of callings, meals, etc.

Historical Analysis

In offering a historical analysis of the Gospel narrative, one affirms that it is plausible from the historical point of view: in other words, more probable than something else. Let us look at that more closely.

1. The account of the calling of Matthew. Applying the most important criteria of historical analysis that we've examined so far, we have:

   a. **The criterion of multiple testimony.** The account appears only in the three synoptics, which is why it is often said to originate with Mark. From that point of view, then, this is not a case of multiple testimony. But the call by Jesus as presented here does satisfy this criterion, for it is presented the same way in many other Gospel passages.

   b. **The criterion of discontinuity and continuity between Judaism and early Christianity.** The teachers of Judaism had disciples: in this there is continuity. But these teachers held forth in the synagogues, and students chose their own teacher of the Law. But Jesus is an itinerant teacher, not chosen by disciples but the one who chooses them, calling them to follow him, not the Law. The primitive Christian community similarly followed the Master's model in acting as it did.

   c. **The criterion of consistency with Jesus' other words and deeds.** The singularity of Jesus—calling people to follow him and not the Law, asking that one leave all things, etc.—is consistent with much else that he says and does: the last of the Beatitudes, the promised inheritance (a hundred for one) of those who leave all for him, his invitation to take up the cross and follow him, etc.

More could be said, but it should be clear that, even if it cannot be demonstrated that the calling of Matthew took place exactly as depicted, it can be shown that the account reflects Jesus' special way of acting, which the Evangelists could not have invented, and which was certainly operative in the call of Matthew.

2. The meal with the publicans and sinners. Here, too, several criteria seem relevant.

a. **Multiple testimony.** That Jesus dined with publicans and sinners is repeated throughout the Gospel. Recall the accusation directed against the Lord before he told the parable of the prodigal son (Lk 15:2) or the reproach that seems to have been common: "For John came neither eating nor drinking, and they say, 'He has a demon'; the Son of man came eating and drinking, and they say, 'Behold, a glutton and a drunkard, a friend of tax collectors and sinners!'" (Mt 11:18–19; cf. Lk 7:33–34).

b. **Continuity and discontinuity with Judaism and with the first Christian communities.** Then, as now, eating together signified a communion of interests, of practices. To eat with sinners—and the publicans were classified with them—could be taken as acceptance of their activities and participation in their faults. Hence the reproach that the Pharisees often directed at our Lord. But the religion of Israel also clearly expressed God's desire to save those who had gone astray. Ezekiel used the image of straying sheep: "I will seek the lost, and I will bring back the strayed, and I will bind up the crippled, and I will strengthen the weak, and the fat and the strong I will watch over; I will feed them in justice" (Ezek 34:16). Jesus, in continuity and discontinuity with the received Tradition, takes the novel step of sharing the table with publicans and sinners in order to move them to conversion.

c. **Consistency.** The call to conversion and table communion with publicans and sinners are consistent with Jesus' singular understanding of his mission: as the fulfillment of the Scriptures of Israel. This understanding affected many things: his position in regard to the Temple, his acceptance of death on the Cross, etc. In his attitude toward publicans and sinners Jesus clearly took the same attitude as God.

So, as above, we cannot prove conclusively that this particular meal with publicans and sinners took place, but we can show this attitude of Jesus was repeated on many occasions. In such circumstances it is more reasonable to believe in the account's historicity than not believe in it.

Finally, we need to consider what redaction criticism adds to our understanding of the Gospels by examining the particular emphases of each Evangelist.

Redaction Analysis

Redaction criticism deals with two things: small differences among the Gospels are examined to make clearer the particular teachings that particular passages aim to communicate; and a passage's relationship to the general plan of its Gospel is probed for its significance.

We can see the first of these questions at work in the synoptic schema laid out above. Note that some of the variations are italicized. Now let us look at each Evangelist in turn.

Mark. Mark gets the fewest italics, indicating the fewest variations. This could mean that he was the source for the other two Gospels, whose writers expanded their texts with additional material. Or it could mean the three Gospels have a common source: in which case it is usually said that Mark modified it the least. The important point in any case, as the italics indicate, is Mark's style—his narrative's spontaneity and liking for details. So we get in the explanation, "the son of Alphaeus," along with stylistic touches (a bit cluttered) that the other two Evangelists simplify, making their accounts smoother but less lively.

As for the second point—situating the meaning of the passage in relation to the Gospel as a whole—recall the importance of discipleship in Mark's narrative. In his Gospel, this passage comes at the beginning of the public life of Jesus. In the first three chapters of St. Mark, Jesus, along with his preaching and cures, promptly chooses disciples who accompany him and associate themselves with his mission. Having told of the calls of the first four disciples, he now tells of Levi's. Soon he names the twelve as a group.

Matthew. In the first Gospel, what stands out immediately is that the text calls the publican Matthew, and that is the name of one of the twelve, whom the Evangelist calls "Matthew, the publican" (Mt 10:3). It seems that the author of the first Gospel has reasons to identify the two; and this is one of the reasons internal to the Gospel which support the thesis that Matthew is the author of this text.

In the third and fourth paragraphs of each Gospel, we see that Matthew, like Luke, gives a simpler version than St. Mark without omitting anything essential.

In the fifth paragraph, the Pharisees ask the disciples why their "master" eats with publicans and sinners. Remember that St. Matthew emphasizes the character of Jesus as a teacher: his is the teaching Gospel. If, moreover, we recall that Matthew's readers live with many non-Christian Jews, it becomes clear that he is contrasting Jesus' teaching as teacher of Christians with the teachings of the Jewish teachers.

This same contrast, though operative on a deeper level, emerges in the case of the phrase italicized in the final paragraph: "Go and learn what this means, 'I desire mercy, and not sacrifice.'" It appears only one other time in the whole of the New Testament, in Matthew 12:7, and there also in the context of a controversy with the Pharisees. The phrase comes from the book of Hosea, but it was much used by the Jews after the destruction of the Temple of Jerusalem by Titus in the year 70. Jewish sources tell this anecdote of Yojanan ben Zakkay, the rabbi who founded the Jewish community in Yamnia, near Tel Aviv, after Jerusalem had been destroyed:

"This happened to Rabi Yojanan ben Zakkay who was traveling when R. Yehosua came running behind him and said: 'Woe is us! The house of our lives [the Temple] has been destroyed, the place where we made expiation for our sins.' He answered: 'Don't fear, we have another expiation in its place.' He was asked: 'What is it?' The answer was: 'I desire mercy and not sacrifice'"(Hosea 6:6) (Abot de Rabi Natan, B, 8). May we suppose that St. Matthew, in evoking the words of Jesus, is supplying arguments to the Christians now in conflict with Jews, to show them that what they now teach is just what Jesus taught and their predecessors scorned?

In the entire narrative of Matthew, the passage comes after the Sermon on the Mount. In that discourse Jesus is presented as the supreme legislator. In the events of chapters 8 and 9 he is shown as the Messiah who guarantees his doctrine by the miracles that confirm his authority. This passage depicts Jesus conducting himself with such authority.

Luke. St. Luke adds the most details, always in brief notes. In the second paragraph he says Levi "left everything"—*relictis omnibus*, in the Vulgate—and followed Jesus. Peter, Andrew, and the Sons of Zebedee also "left everything" (Lk 5:11) and followed Jesus. As we have seen when considering the "new man" theme of this Gospel, following Christ means decisively leaving what one has and trusting solely in God. This feature, common to the whole of the third Gospel, is present here.

In the third paragraph, Luke says the meal was at Levi's house. In this way he eliminates the possibility of confusion arising from the statements of the other two Evangelists who write "in his house" without specifying whether this means Jesus' (Peter's) house or Matthew's.

Like Matthew, Luke avoids the repetition found in the third and fourth paragraphs of Mark.

Also proper to Luke is precision in the use of medical terms. This does not come through in the English translation, although Matthew and Mark use the term "strong" rather than "healthy" for those who do not need a doctor.

Luke also adds some doctrinal precisions. Jesus' words in the last sentence express his mission more correctly: he has come to call sinners "to repentance," so that they may convert. There is a certain ambiguity in Jesus' words as Matthew and Mark give them: he might be saying, "If you are already just, why are you upset?" But the ambiguity disappears in Luke, where we are given a clear exposition of doctrine: Jesus came to call people to conversion, to penance.

There also is this difference between Luke and the other two, that in St. Luke the accusation of eating with publicans and sinners is directed not to Jesus but his disciples. The explanation may lie in the "vital context" (*Sitz im Leben*) of the preaching and the Gospel's composition. St. Luke says explicitly that the meal was in Levi's house, and that Jesus' mission is to lead sinners to repentance. The point may be that disciples, like their Master, can and should share their table with publicans and sinners in order to lead them to conversion; but this does not imply inviting them to the "Table in the House of the Lord"—that is, making them participants of the Eucharist. Recall that Luke was written in Corinth or nearby in Achaia, and then think of the Eucharistic abuses denounced by St. Paul in his letter to the Corinthians (1 Cor 11:18–34).

The relationship of this passage to the Gospel as a whole is not of great importance in Luke. He uses the same framework as Mark in telling how Jesus progressively formed the group of disciples in a process culminating in the choice of the twelve apostles.

By now it should be clear how the Gospels embody history and teaching at the same time. This in turn suggests how the Gospel can be read with greater understanding and profit. Let us now consider another text: the Baptism of Jesus in the Jordan.

2. The Baptism of Jesus in the Jordan

Let us begin by looking at the text itself:

Mt 3:13–17	Mk 1:9–11	Lk 3:21–22
13 Then Jesus came from Galilee to the Jordan to John, to be baptized by him. 14 John would have prevented him, saying, "I need to be baptized by you, and do you come to me?" 15 But Jesus answered him, "Let it be so now; for thus it is fitting for us to fulfill all righteousness." Then he consented.	9 In those days Jesus came from Nazareth of Galilee	21 Now when all the people were baptized,
16 And when Jesus was baptized, he went up immediately from the water, and behold, the heavens were opened and he saw the Spirit of God descending like a dove, and alighting on him; 17 and lo, a voice from heaven, saying, "This is my beloved Son, with whom I am well pleased."	and was baptized by John in the Jordan. 10 And when he came up out of the water, immediately he saw the heavens opened and the Spirit descending upon him like a dove; 11 and a voice came from heaven, "Thou art my beloved Son; with thee I am well pleased."	and when Jesus also had been baptized and was praying, the heaven was opened, 22 and the Holy Spirit descended upon him in bodily form, as a dove, and a voice came from heaven, "Thou art my beloved Son; with thee I am well pleased."

Historical Examination

It seems to be a historical fact that Jesus went to John to be baptized. All four Gospels narrate this episode (Mt 3:13–17; Mk 1:9–11; Lk 3: 21–22; cf. Jn 1:32–34), and other parts of the New Testament also testify to it (Acts 4:27; 10:38) as do extra-canonical texts such as the Gospel of the Ebionites and that of the Nazarenes.

This same Gospel tradition also affirms, however, that John preached "a baptism of repentance for the forgiveness of sins. And there went out to him all the country of Judea, and all the people of Jerusalem; and they were baptized by him in the river Jordan, confessing their sins" (Mk 1:4–5). So what was the significance of Jesus' baptism? Christian faith holds him to have been sinless (cf. Heb 4:15: ". . . one who in every respect has been tempted as we are, yet without sin"); as such, he had no need for John's baptism.

The answer requires that we examine two things: Jesus' actions and the significance given to this episode by the Evangelists.

Historical actions. It is clear from the Old Testament that confession of sins in Scripture does not mean publicly announcing one's specific offenses. It has two aspects instead: first, publicly confessing that one has separated oneself from God; and most important, solidarity with the sins of the others. So, for example, the Old Testament tells of Ezra's prayer for forgiveness, even though he had not participated in the sins of Israel that he confessed before God.

> At the evening sacrifice I rose from my fasting, with my garments and my mantle rent, and fell upon my knees and spread out my hands to the LORD my God, saying:
>
> > "O my God, I am ashamed and blush to lift my face to thee, my God, for our iniquities have risen higher than our heads, and our guilt has mounted up to the heavens. From the days

of our fathers to this day we have been in great guilt; and for our iniquities we, our kings, and our priests have been given into the hand of the kings of the lands, to the sword, to captivity, to plundering, and to utter shame, as at this day. But now for a brief moment favor has been shown by the LORD our God, to leave us a remnant, and to give us a secure hold within his holy place, that our God may brighten our eyes and grant us a little reviving in our bondage. For we are bondmen; yet our God has not forsaken us in our bondage, but has extended to us his steadfast love before the kings of Persia, to grant us some reviving to set up the house of our God, to repair its ruins, and to give us protection in Judea and Jerusalem.

"And now, O our God, what shall we say after this? For we have forsaken thy commandments, which thou didst command by thy servants the prophets, saying, 'The land which you are entering, to take possession of it, is a land unclean with the pollutions of the peoples of the lands, with their abominations which have filled it from end to end with their uncleanness.' And after all that has come upon us for our evil deeds and for our great guilt, seeing that thou, our God, hast punished us less than our iniquities deserved and hast given us such a remnant as this, shall we break thy commandments again and intermarry with the peoples who practice these abominations? Wouldst thou not be angry with us till thou wouldst consume us, so that there should be no remnant, nor any to escape? O Lord, the God of Israel, thou art just, for we are left a remnant that has escaped, as at this day. Behold, we are before thee in our guilt, for none can stand before thee because of this." (Ezra 9:5–15)

In addition, at least some of the early Christians were already conscious of how this gesture of Jesus could be misunderstood. St. Matthew therefore includes the dialogue between Jesus and John which makes it clear that it is John the Baptist, not Jesus, who can consider himself a sinner and feel solidarity with the sins of mankind, and not Jesus. Yet Jesus determines to enter into solidarity with sinful humanity in order to satisfy divine justice, and John therefore assents to his baptism.

The other historical occurrence here is a theophany, a manifestation of God. Rationalistic authors usually dismiss this, saying the account is a myth. This also is how they explain the Transfiguration, the Resurrection, and Jesus' walking on the waters. As we shall see in more detail when considering the miracles, this view expresses an a priori refusal to accept the entry of the supernatural into human history. (Accounts of marvelous actions performed by Jesus are not confined to the Gospels. For example, the second letter of Peter recalls the apostle's testimony concerning the Transfiguration.)

Significance. Apostolic Tradition does not focus so much on the baptism itself as on the theophany which then occurred, with its declaration of Jesus' divine sonship and his mission. Two points in the *Catechism of the Catholic Church* sum up the significance of the baptism.

No. 535 calls the baptism "the manifestation ('Epiphany') of Jesus as Messiah of Israel and Son of God."

No. 536 makes the following points.

1. "The baptism of Jesus is on his part the acceptance and inauguration of his mission as God's suffering Servant. He allows himself to be numbered among sinners; he is already 'the Lamb of God, who takes away the sin of the world' (cf. Is 53:12). Already he is anticipating the 'baptism' of his bloody death (cf. Mk 10:38; Lk 12:50)."

2. "Already he is coming to 'fulfill all righteousness,' that is, he is submitting himself entirely to his Father's will: out of love he consents to this baptism of death for the remission of our sins (cf. Mt 26:39)."

3. "The Father's voice responds to the Son's acceptance, proclaiming his entire delight in his Son (cf. Lk 4:33; Is 42:1). The *Spirit* whom Jesus possessed in fullness from his

conception comes to 'rest on him' (Jn 1:32–33; cf. Is 11:2). Jesus will be the source of the Spirit for all mankind."

4. "At his baptism *'the heavens were opened'* (Mt 3:16)— *the heavens that Adam's sin had closed*—and the waters were sanctified by the descent of Jesus and the Spirit, a prelude to the new creation."

The matter becomes clearer when we examine some common expressions of the Gospel tradition echoing the Old Testament texts.

1. "The heavens were opened (torn open)." The expression goes back to Isaiah 64:1, which recalls the cry of the exiles in Babylonia awaiting the restoration of Israel: "O that thou wouldst rend the heavens and come down." This is a plea for the restoration of the People of God, with God living in their midst. It is fulfilled in Jesus. The opening up of heaven also evokes the abolition of the boundary between heaven and earth, which, as Jacob's dream in Bethel indicates (Gen 28:16–19), takes place in the Temple. Man's path to heaven is Jesus Christ.

2. "The Holy Spirit descended upon him . . . as a dove." The Spirit always comes in the context of mission. And the messiah King (Is 11:1–10) has the gifts of the Spirit. But the most important text is found at the beginning of the first Servant of God poem of Isaiah (42:1): "Behold my servant, whom I uphold, my chosen, in whom my soul delights; I have put my Spirit upon him, he will bring forth justice to the nations." Clearly, Isaiah is pointing to the descent of the Spirit, who shows Jesus his mission while the Father's voice from heaven declares him to be "well pleased."

3. Jesus is "my beloved Son." As we saw in connection with the Gospel of St. Matthew, in the New Testament Jesus is called the Son of God. But this is not simply the sum total

of the Old Testament references. The process is rather the reverse. As Son of God, Jesus assumes a mission others should have carried out. He is the Son of God, and is the beloved one. This expression (*agapetos*) also appears on other occasions, such as at the Transfiguration; but above all it appears in the parable of the murderous vine-yard workers, in which Jesus refers to God, to Israel, and obviously to himself as represented by the beloved son murdered outside the city.

Let us consider now how each Evangelist handles these several aspects.

The Editing of the Gospels

Mark. Mark often writes from Jesus' point of view. It is Jesus who "came" from Galilee, "was baptized," who "saw" the heavens opened, to whom the voice speaks: "You are my beloved Son, with you I am well pleased." The focus is upon Jesus, what he does, sees, hears. Thus, as one might expect, what emerges in this episode are his identity and mission. This is clear from the use of nearly the same formula as in the Transfiguration: "This is my beloved Son; listen to him" (Mk 9:7).

Considered in this light, "You are my beloved Son, with you I am well pleased" could be understood as Jesus' discovery of his inmost self (Son of God) and vocation, as well as confirmation of what he already knows or God's sign that his mission is now to begin. Some minimalist exegetes have sought to show from this that Mark is an adoptionist (the baptism at the Jordan marks Jesus' adoption as Son of God) as Matthew and Luke are generationists (Jesus is God's Son through generation by the Holy Spirit in the womb of the Virgin), and John adopts a transcendent point of view (Jesus is the eternal Word of God become flesh). This, however, is simply clever but rash speculation. What Mark does make clear is that upon Jesus' acceptance of his mission, it was confirmed from heaven.

Matthew. The variations in Matthew serve to remove any doubt that Mark might leave. We have already seen this in regard to Jesus' dialogue with the Baptist, and now we see it again. "The heavens were opened" emphasizes Jesus' majesty and suggests his divinity, as does the voice from heaven—now directed to the bystanders: "This is my beloved Son, with whom I am well pleased." In sum, the episode is an epiphany: Jesus is shown as God.

Luke. Luke does not mention John the Baptist. This points to an idea frequently repeated in his Gospel and in the Acts of the Apostles: the phases and times of salvation. The prophets held the stage until John; after him, a new era has begun.

Here, too, we find something else typical of Luke: Jesus is shown praying. This motif recurs in Luke at other crucial moments: before the apostles are chosen, at Caesarea Philippi, on the cross, etc.

Finally, Luke speaks of a bodily descent by the Spirit upon Jesus. Luke also is the one who quotes Jesus as saying to his disciples after the Resurrection, "See my hands and my feet, that it is I myself; handle me, and see; for a spirit has not flesh and bones as you see that I have" (Lk 24:39). In the present passage, St. Luke may be noting the corporeality of the Spirit's descent as a way of emphasizing that it was no illusion.

3. CONCLUSION

Much more could be said, but the point should be clear: Attentive reading of the Gospel in the light of what is already known (from other reading, from other passages of Scripture, etc.) can enrich our understanding of what the Holy Spirit and the apostolic proclamation of the Good News wish to communicate to us.

9

The Miracles of Jesus

Juan Chapa

The miracles of Jesus can be considered from several different points of view. The present treatment is eminently exegetical, beginning with historical-critical questions useful for a better understanding of the Gospel texts and a firmer foundation of faith in Jesus Christ, while at the same time responding to contemporary Christological challenges. The International Theological Commission's words are relevant here:

> In our days the problem of Jesus Christ has been posed with renewed keenness, both on the plane of piety and of theology. The study of Sacred Scripture and the historical research carried out on the great Christological councils have brought us many new elements. Men and women today present, with renewed insistence, the questions of the past: Who then, is this man? (cf. Lk 7:49) Where do these gifts come from? What wisdom is this that has been granted to him? What is the meaning of the miracles carried out through his hands? (Mk 6:2) It is clear that in certain circles, a response that remains on the level of the general study of the science of religions is not adequate.[1]

Let us begin with what has been said in recent years about Jesus' miracles and their historicity. Then we shall look at their significance in the Gospels.

---

1. Our translation; for official English text see: International Theological Commission: Texts and Documents (1969–1985), San Francisco: Ignatius Press, 1989.

1. HISTORICITY OF THE MIRACLE NARRATIVES

The accounts of miracles in the Gospels began to be questioned systematically by the pseudo-scientific ideology of the eighteenth and nineteenth centuries. More recently, however, there has been a shift from the skepticism of literary interpretations common throughout much of the twentieth century, which viewed the community as the source of the Gospel traditions, to a renewed appreciation of the historicity of miracle accounts.

Recent studies concerning the historical Jesus, apparently assigning less weight than before to anti-Christian philosophical prejudices yet still strongly influenced by positivistic presuppositions, have established the value of New Testament as history. As a result, it is common today to see Jesus as a miracle worker and exorcist. A large number of exegetes, operating as historians, have abandoned skepticism in favor of the affirmation—probable for some, certain for others—that Jesus worked miracles. The impulse to destroy the "myth" of Jesus as a worker of miracles has largely collapsed. But understandings of what a "miracle" is vary greatly, and some writers continue to view them from an obviously rationalistic perspective.

Thus, in light of the developments of recent decades, today's scholarship concurs that it can be shown that Jesus performed miracles, that they were numerous, and that he performed them with a specific meaning in view. This concurrence is not the result of sentimentalism but of methodical historical research. Let us look at this more closely.

Jesus as a Miracle Worker

A dispassionate view of the Gospels obliges one to conclude that Jesus performed miracles and gave them a very special meaning. In a classic work on Jesus' miracles, Father René Latourelle writes: "It is therefore arbitrary to claim that the miracle stories are the result of an activity of the Church, which is alone responsible for their form and meaning. Quite the contrary: the meaning precedes the story and has its origin in Jesus. It is pre-paschal. The tradition has simply accepted this pre-paschal meaning that goes back to Jesus, opened it up, as it were, and gone into it more deeply."[2] This simply endorses the testimony of Peter, as recounted by St. Luke in the Acts of the Apostles.

> Men of Israel, hear these words: Jesus of Nazareth, *a man attested to you by God with mighty works and wonders and signs which God did through him in your midst*, as you yourselves know—this Jesus, delivered up according to the definite plan and foreknowledge of God, you crucified and killed by the hands of lawless men. (Acts 2:22–23)

Peter's words sum up Jesus' actions as transmitted in the early Church. They present Jesus as a miracle worker, as the Gospel narratives confirm.

Testimony of the miracle-working activity of Jesus. The Gospels testify that Jesus performed miracles and that there were many of them. Consider the episode of Jesus' "failure" as a teacher or prophet in the cities of Chorazain, Bethsaida, and Capernaum. Here Jesus is not believed despite his miracles.

> "Woe to you, Chorazain! woe to you, Bethsaida! for if the mighty works done in you had been done in Tyre and Sidon, they would have repented long ago in sackcloth and ashes. But I tell you, it shall be more tolerable on the day of judgment for Tyre and Sidon than for you. And you, Capernaum, will you be exalted to heaven? You shall be brought down to Hades. For if the mighty works done in you had been done in Sodom, it would have remained until this day. But I tell you that it shall be more tolerable on the day of judgment for the land of Sodom than for you." (Mt 11:21–24; cf. Lk 10:13–15)

---

2. *The Miracles of Jesus and the Theology of Miracles*, New York: Paulist Press, 1988, 41.

The evidence for the authenticity of this passage includes its style, its consistency, its tone of reproach, etc. What stands out especially, however, is that the evangelical tradition records the apparent failure of Jesus, even though the early Christians believed very firmly in his power (cf. Acts 2:22; 10:38). Why, then, would they preserve the memory of an incident in which he was rejected despite his miracles? The only possible explanation is that it was a historical fact—it really happened. Also reflected here are elements of Jesus' pre-paschal message: the call to conversion and his miracles. But the text also tells us something else in that it speaks of *miracles* in these two cities, while the Gospel narratives do not tell of a miracle in Chorozain and speaks of only one in Bethsaida (Mk 8:22). Evidently, then, more miracles than those reported in the Gospels were known to the tradition.

Another, similar text showing Jesus' power to expel demons at work reports a controversy with certain Pharisees over that power's origin. An accusation against Jesus is recalled in the course of it.

> Then a blind and dumb demoniac was brought to him, and he healed him, so that the dumb man spoke and saw. And all the people were amazed, and said, "Can this be the Son of David?" But when the Pharisees heard it they said, "It is only by Beelzebul, the prince of demons, that this man casts out demons." Knowing their thoughts, he said to them, "Every kingdom divided against itself is laid waste, and no city or house divided against itself will stand; and if Satan casts out Satan, he is divided against himself; how then will his kingdom stand? And if I cast out demons by Beelzebul, by whom do your sons cast them out? Therefore they shall be your judges. But if it is by the Spirit of God that I cast out demons, then the kingdom of God has come upon you." (Mt 12:22–28)

It is inconceivable that the Christian community should have invented this episode. What possible reason could there be to dream up such a story and make it a part of the Gospel? Yet in its own way it makes it clear that Jesus did expel demons, for the argument recorded here is not about whether he did it but by what power it was done. The first Christians understood that Jesus was conscious of being Satan's conqueror.[3]

This tradition about Jesus' performance of miracles can be confirmed from other sources. There was in antiquity no doubt about Jesus' existence. On the contrary, pains were taken to preserve the testimony of witnesses who claimed that Jesus deceived the people by doing magic: for example, an anonymous *baraita*,[4] probably of the second century, relates Jesus' condemnation on the eve of the Passover for deceiving Israel by practicing witchcraft. Similar accusations of magic were made against Jesus by Celsus in the second century and were refuted by Origen. There are allusions to them in St. Justin, Arnobius, and Lactantius.

All of this constitutes historical evidence that Jesus was known for working miracles. Without the miracles, there is no way to explain either the enthusiasm of the crowds and the disciples or the hatred of his enemies.

The accounts of miracles transmitted in the Gospels. The references in the Gospel narratives to miracles that Jesus performed are very abundant. In Mark, nearly a third of the text—209 out of 666 verses—gives accounts of miracles. The proportion is less in the other two synoptics, and in St. John's

---

3. Many other Gospel texts relate this activity of Jesus: see Mt 11:5–7; 21–23; Lk 13:31.

4. The *baraitas* are oral traditions of rabbinic Judaism, not collected in the Mishna (first collection of traditions made between the second and third centuries A.D.) but in the Talmud (a more ample collection made in the fifth century). The *baraita* here referred to is in the Babylonian Talmud, Sanedrin 43. There is a similar one in Sanedrin 107b.

Gospel there are only seven miracles (two of the twenty-nine that are related in the synoptics and five of his own). But these seven are of great consequence in the fourth Gospel—so much so that its first part often is called the "Book of the Signs."

More than twenty years passed between the occurrence of the miraculous events and their being written down (in the Gospel of Mark). Moreover, the Evangelists are in greater agreement about what Jesus said than what he did (after all, it is more difficult to describe deeds than transmit words). But even so, it is very possible that descriptions of miracles already existed which the Evangelists used in composing their works. Today therefore it is agreed that many of these accounts of cures and exorcisms reflect the recollections of eyewitnesses. Details vary, but the fundamental facts are certain. And it is logical and natural that, if Jesus performed cures and exorcisms, some would be preserved and transmitted in the memories of people who saw these things happen. This is not a product of some myth-making impulse regarding Jesus on the part of the early Church.

In the preaching of the apostles, from which the Gospels are primarily derived, the early Christians heard the accounts from the lips of eyewitnesses of the extraordinary events in recent times and, therefore, something that could be checked under the aspect that we might call critical-historical, so that it is not surprising that they were inserted in the Gospels.[5]

In verifying the authenticity of the Gospel concerning Jesus' miracles it is customary to use the criteria noted above regarding the historical character of the Gospels. So, for example, the criterion of *multiple attestation* is applied to the miracle of the multiplication of the loaves recounted in the synoptics and in St. John. The criterion of *discontinuity* emphasizes the originality of Jesus' attitude: he performs miracles in his own

---

5. Pope John Paul II, Audience, December 2, 1987 (Vatican Web site).

name and under his own authority, unlike the prophets of the Old Testament, the apostles (who acted in Jesus' name), and other wonder workers of the time (Apollonius, Hanina ben Dosa, exorcists). The criterion of *consistency* has both an *external* and *internal* sense. The external sense refers to the harmony between the account and the contemporary milieu, as, for example, the name or identity of a sick person or the one who represents him or her (as in the case of Peter's mother-in-law), or the name of the place where the miracle occurred (e.g., Jericho). The internal sense concerns the miracles' link to the proclamation of the Kingdom, a fundamental element of Jesus' pre-paschal teaching.

There are other criteria as well, but this suggests their nature and function. Applying them to the miracle accounts supplies convincing historical evidence.

2. The Meaning of Jesus' Miracles

The significance of miracles in the Old Testament tradition provides a framework for understanding Jesus' miracles.

Old Testament miracles were typically seen as "prodigies" (*mofet*), "signs" (*ot*), or "works" (*maaseh*). These terms were translated into Greek as, respectively, *terata, semeia,* and *erga* (or *dynameis*). The Hebrew concept underlying the words presupposes that there is no difference between natural and supernatural. God's power has no limits; nothing is impossible for him. What he does can be done in an ordinary way or an extraordinary one through a divine intervention, both for a particular purpose and to manifest the power of God.

For the Israelites, God's greatest prodigy and most marvelous sign—his most remarkable work—lay in forming his people and exercising his providence on their behalf, including the portents that accompanied their liberation from Egypt and their journey to the Promised Land. God intervenes in history, correcting its course by means of miracles, sometimes in response to men's faith. At certain moments, therefore, we witness a cluster of miracles, as it were: above all, at the time of the Exodus and again at the coming of the Kingdom of God.

The New Testament reflects this. Some distinguish here three aspects of the miraculous: (1) a deed perceived as a prodigy, an extraordinary thing (*terata*); (2) an expression of power to do what the miracle accomplishes (*dynamis*); (3) a sign that is an invitation to live in a new way (*semeia*). The miracle interrupts the ordinary course of things, and moves one who witnesses it to inquire into the identity of the one who performs it and to identify with the cause it serves.

In his discourse at Pentecost St. Peter refers to what Jesus said and did, alluding to these three aspects: "Jesus of Nazareth, a man attested to you by God with mighty works and wonders and signs" (*dynamesi kai terasi kai semeiois*, Acts 2:22). He shows how the miracles are marvelous exercises of the power of God and signs of another reality, the arrival of the Kingdom. They point to the divine omnipotence and to God's salvific power impelling people toward faith.

The synoptics tend to speak of a miracle as *dynamis*—force or power—or else focus on the marvelous aspect, terming Jesus' works *thaumasia* or *terata*, "astonishing things." The emphasis is on Jesus' power, which testifies to his messiahship, and on the extraordinary character of those events as eyewitnessed by those who saw them or heard of them from others. St. John, on the other hand, calls the miracles *semeia*, "signs." The expression indicates that the most important thing about these works is that they point to something else—they manifest God at work; and Jesus is the Christ, the Son of God.

Context and Originality

In Jesus' day certain people were known for performing prodigies. Jesus, however, worked far more miracles, and with very different meaning from the prodigies some of his contemporaries may have performed (supposing they really did). The number of miracles attributed to these others is very small, but in the Gospels there are nineteen accounts of miracles in Matthew, eighteen in Mark, twenty in Luke, and eight in John. The synoptics and John also refer to the many other miracles Jesus performed (cf. Mk 1:32–34 and parallel; 3:7–12 and par.; 6:53–56; Jn 20:30).

The meaning of Jesus' miracles is also different. The cures of Asclepios (Esculapius), in which priests who practiced medicine took part and which on many occasions seemed extravagant, did not seek moral change in those cured. But Jesus worked miracles that pointed to recognition of the goodness of God and change of life in those who were benefitted. The cures of Apollonius are recounted to show that the philosopher was a model of wisdom and deserving of honor, whereas Jesus appeared reluctant to work miracles because he did not seek his own glory. A taste for the marvelous and an easy triumph apart from the cross were not to his liking (Mk 8:11–12; Jn 6:30–31; Mt 16:4; Lk 23:8). The marvels of Hanina and other Galileans underlined their piety, their status as objects of God's blessing, and God's granting of the miracle in response to prayer. In Jesus' case, however, it is he who works the miracle by his own authority.

In sum, characteristics of Jesus' miracle-working activity are their great *number*, his reluctance to perform them indicating that he did not seek his own glory, and especially the *meaning* he gave them. Note also that the accounts of his miracles are notable for their *sobriety* and the absence of any desire to exaggerate the figure of Jesus.

Classification

The Gospel miracles traditionally are divided into those that concern Jesus (the Transfiguration and Resurrection) and those he performs. The latter include miracles in reference to persons and miracles in reference to nature. The consensus these days, however, is that these categories are not very helpful inasmuch as miracles always manifest God's action and, whether they affect people or nature, always show forth the power of Jesus. Thus the tendency now is to classify miracles according to the form they take. Some suggest the following:

- **Exorcisms.** They manifest the inner reality of the Kingdom of God, liberation from sin and Satan.

- **Cures.** They exhibit the exterior aspect of the Kingdom of God, liberation from sickness and death. They include the three resurrections (the daughter of Jairus, the son of the widow of Nain, Lazarus).

- **Miracles of giving.** Jesus intervenes to benefit people experiencing the lack of something material (the multiplication of the loaves, the wedding feast at Cana, the miraculous catch of fish).

- **Miracles of deliverance.** Jesus intervenes to save one or more persons in a critical situation (calming the tempest).

- **Miracles of legitimation.** These are cures that justify Jesus' behavior while having a somewhat controversial character (e.g., the cure of the stooped woman).

- **Epiphanies.** For example, the Transfiguration and the appearances of the risen Christ.

Meaning

Exegetes agree on three aspects that mark Jesus' activity as a miracle worker.

1. Jesus' miracles find their meaning in the context of the Kingdom of God: "If it is by the Spirit of God that I cast out demons, then the kingdom of God has come upon you" (Mt 12:28). Jesus inaugurates the Kingdom; miracles are a call to a response of faith. Kingdom and miracles are inseparable.

2. The miracles are not accomplished by techniques (as might be the case with a doctor) or the involvement of demons or angels (as with a magician). They are brought about by the supernatural power of the Spirit of God.

3. Jesus worked miracles (especially cures) on those who had faith and accepted the proclamation of the Kingdom. In John nevertheless one also finds accounts in which faith is a consequence of a miracle worked on Jesus' initiative.

To this we might add:

• Miracles in regard to nature are signs that the divine power at work in Jesus extends beyond the human world and involves dominion over the forces of nature.

• Miracles of curing and exorcisms are signs that Jesus has power to save man from the evil that threatens his soul.

• Some miracles point to other spiritual realities. Bodily cures—liberation from the slavery of infirmity—signify the soul's release from the slavery of sin. The expulsion of demons expresses Christ's victory over evil. The multiplication of the loaves suggests the gift of the Eucharist. The calming of the tempest is an invitation to trust in Christ in difficult moments. The resurrection of Lazarus shows that Christ is the resurrection itself; it points to the final resurrection.

• Jesus' miracles are signs that confirm his Messianic mission and the coming of the Kingdom of God. They are linked to the call to faith: either because faith is a condition for the performance of the miracle, or because the miracle elicits faith in those who experience it or witness it. Jesus declined to work miracles in the face of a lack of faith (Mk 6:1–6; Mt 13:54–58; Mt 16:20; Mk 9:29).

The miracles are above all Jesus' way of showing that the Kingdom of God has arrived. This also is the conclusion of traditional apologetics, which emphasizes the miracles' purpose of showing the power of Christ—that is, demonstrating his authenticity and the truth of his teaching. The First Vatican Council included miracles with prophecies and the Church among Christianity's motives of credibility: "They are most sure signs of revelation and adapted to the intelligence of everyone" (*De Fide Catholica*, ch. 3; DS 3009).

From these considerations we can conclude as follows:

1. A miracle is a work of God—he is its author. Through miracles he shows his love and goodness. But Jesus is the one who performs miracles, which thus testify to him as bearer of revelation and salvation. Miracles (especially in Luke) are signs of God's mercy toward the afflicted and sorrowful.

2. A miracle establishes a personal bond with Jesus that transforms the person on whose behalf the miracle was worked. He or she participates in the miracle through faith in Jesus: "Rise and go your way; your faith has made you well" (Lk 17:19). Being cured is linked with being saved.

3. A miracle is a moment of choice. The person can welcome Jesus and be converted, or close himself off from him. The purpose is not to awe or astonish the person, but to invite him to enter into dialogue with God. The outcome depends on his decision. We see this, for example, in the cure of the two blind men, when Jesus says: "Do you believe that I am able to do this?" (Mt 9:28).

4. A miracle is a sign of the divine gifts offered to men through the grace of Christ. In the Gospel of John, Jesus' miracles reveal the mystery of the sacramental economy, particularly baptism (the cure of the paralytic, John 5, and of the man born blind, John 9) and the Eucharist (the multiplication of the loaves).

5. The miracle is directed to the salvation of the whole man, body and soul. People imprisoned by the power of evil and sickness have lost their freedom and dignity; in curing the sick and those possessed by the devil, Jesus restores to them the dignity of God's children. The account of the cure of the possessed man of Gerasa expresses this with precision. He recovers his dignity and is left "clothed and in his right mind," at home with friends and relatives (Mk 5:15, 19).

6. The miracle has an ecclesial character. Jesus gives to his disciples power to perform miracles: "Preach as you go, saying, 'The kingdom of heaven is at hand.' Heal the sick, raise the dead, cleanse lepers, cast out demons" (Mt 10:7–8). After his resurrection, that power is present in the Church: "Now many signs and wonders were done among the people by the hands of the apostles" (Acts 5:12). Here is a sign of the universal salvation that the Good News announces (cf. Mk 16:15–18).

7. Miracles also have an eschatological meaning. In his person Jesus unites hope of final salvation and its present realization. With Jesus, the Kingdom of God breaks into history: "If it is by the Spirit of God that I cast out demons, then the kingdom of God has come upon you" (Mt 12:28). Jesus' miracles anticipate the eschatological destiny of humanity, in full communion with God. They are the brief glimpses of future glory.

Briefly, then, the miracles of Jesus manifest the mystery of his Person. The Kingdom of God is present in his very being.

3. How each Evangelist Presents the Miracles

In light of the situation of each Evangelist at the time of writing his Gospel and each one's intention in regard to his particular audience, the narrative of a particular miracle can have a different doctrinal point in view depending on which Evangelist is presenting it. This is clear with regard to the miracle of the calming of the storm (see the table below).

1. **St. Matthew.** Recall that Jesus is presented here as the Messiah who carries out Messianic works, the suffering Servant of the Lord who takes upon himself our infirmities, and the Lord of the community of the Church, which he makes a participant in his power. In Matthew, faith precedes the miracle. His account is usually schematic, with dialogue central to it. Usually there is a close relation between what is asked and what is granted.

   These characteristics are present in the calming of the storm. The episode's context is the following of Jesus by his disciples.

Mt 8:23–27	Mk 4:3–41	Lk 8:22–25
23 And when he got into the boat, his disciples followed him. 24 And behold, there arose a great storm on the sea, so that the boat was being swamped by the waves; but he was asleep. 25 And they went and woke him, saying, "Save, Lord; we are perishing." 26 And he said to them, "Why are you afraid, O men of little faith?" Then he rose and rebuked the winds and the sea; and there was a	35 On that day, when evening had come, he said to them, "Let us go across to the other side." 36 And leaving the crowd, they took him with them in the boat, just as he was. And other boats were with him. 37 And a great storm of wind arose, and the waves beat into the boat, so that the boat was already filling. 38 But he was in the stern, asleep on the cushion; and they	22 One day he got into a boat with his disciples, and he said to them, "Let us go across to the other side of the lake." So they set out, 23 and as they sailed he fell asleep. And a storm of wind came down on the lake, and they were filling with water, and were in danger. 24 And they went and woke him, saying, "Master, Master, we are perishing!" And he awoke and rebuked cont'd.

Mt 8:23–27 cont'd.	Mk 4:3–41 cont'd.	Lk 8:22–25 cont'd.
great calm. 27 And the men marveled, saying, "What sort of man is this, that even winds and sea obey him?"	woke him and said to him, "Teacher, do you not care if we perish?" 39 And he awoke and rebuked the wind, and said to the sea, "Peace! Be still!" And the wind ceased, and there was a great calm. 40 He said to them, "Why are you afraid? Have you no faith?" 41 And they were filled with awe, and said to one another, "Who then is this, that even wind and sea obey him?"	the wind and the raging waves; and they ceased, and there was a calm. 25 He said to them, "Where is your faith?" And they were afraid, and they marveled, saying to one another, "Who then is this, that he commands even wind and water, and they obey him?"

They still have little faith; therefore, before working the miracle (and not after, as in the other two synoptics) by rebuking the wind and the sea, Jesus reproaches them for that. Here as elsewhere it is evident why the Gospel of St. Matthew is often called the "ecclesiastical Gospel." The miracle teaches something about Jesus' action in the Church: the disciples' boat (v. 23) is the Church, buffeted by the waves of the world and awash in difficulties. Christians sometimes may think Jesus is asleep (v. 24), because they forget that Christ is the Lord (v. 25). But he is the one who controls the world and history. Our firm faith "awakens" him, and then he acts (v. 26) provoking the wonderment of all mankind— "the men" (v. 27) can be understood as those outside the Church—who will accept him.

2. **St. Mark.** Here Jesus performs prodigies as others in those days might have done, but he acts by his own power. Even more than Matthew, Mark emphasizes faith's role in bringing about miracles. Through them Jesus manifests the coming of the Kingdom, so that they serve as a setting for his warfare against Satan. They show his power at work. Hence the many exorcisms.

   The calming of the storm reflects all this. In Mark the context includes Jesus' identity and power. The "sea" (v. 39) refers not only to the lake, but, consistent with an Old Testament tradition, a place of evil forces that only God can dominate, dwelling place of the sea monsters, Leviathan and Rahab (cf. Ps 65:7; 93:4; 107:23–30). In subduing the sea—"Peace! Be still!"—as he does the demons, Jesus shows himself to possess divine power. Hence the disciples' question (v. 41). The miracle is, then, an exorcism, confirming the coming of the Kingdom and Jesus' triumph over the devil.

3. **St. Luke.** The third Gospel's seven miracles are concerned above all with illustrating the word of Jesus the Savior. They show him as a great prophet in the manner of Elijah and Elisha, who worked similar miracles (e.g., Elijah's raising of the son of the widow of Sareptha or Elisha's multiplication of the loaves: cf. 1 Kings 17:17–24; 2 Kings 4:42–44). But above all they are calls to salvation with the cure a sign of salvation.

   Here the miracle of the calming of the storm is a small drama. Jesus' reproach (v. 25) is less severe than in the other two Evangelists, thus emphasizing the majesty of our Lord. Notable, too, is the title by which the disciples call on Jesus: "Master" (v. 24). The expression is not far removed from prophet, and at the same time is connected to the reference to "fear" (v. 25). The fear of those who witness a miracle appears again at the cure of the possessed man of Gerasa, which all three synoptics relate after the episode of the storm. St. Luke is the only one who gives a reason why the inhabitants of the region petition Jesus to leave: "they were seized with great fear" (v. 37). This emphasizes his power and role as a prophet, as also at the raising of the son of the widow of Nain: "Fear seized them all; and they glorified God, saying, 'A great prophet has arisen among us!' and 'God has visited his people!'" (Lk 7:16).

4. **St. John.** The author refers to the miracles as *semeia* (signs) and *erga* (works). They show Jesus to be the Son of God. The principal difference from the synoptics concerns the situation of faith at the time of the miracle. In John, faith follows the event—the miracle is a means given people to come to faith. Miracles have an apologetical significance in that they confirm Jesus' mission and his status as one who exists and acts in union with the Father. They also display his divine glory.

There is in John no parallel to the account of the calming of the storm. Rather, some of the special characteristics of the fourth Gospel can be seen in the miracle of loaves and fishes (cf. the parallel passages below). What stands out in John are:

- The role of Jesus in the miracle: he takes the initiative, conscious of what is about to happen (v. 6), invites the people to the meal, distributes the loaves and the fishes (vv. 6, 11), and directs that what is left over be collected so that nothing is wasted (v. 12).

- The importance of the "bread" (the term appears five times) and the reference to the Passover feast (v. 1). This introduces the discourse about the bread of heaven, the Eucharist, which follows.

- The crowd's failed attempt to seize him and make him king (vv. 14–15). This underlines the fact that the miracle does not have a messianic-political purpose.

Mk 6:30–44	Jn 6:1–15
30 The apostles returned to Jesus, and told him all that they had done and taught. 31 And he said to them, "Come away by yourselves to a lonely place, and rest a while." For many were coming and going, and they had no leisure even to eat. 32 And they went away in the boat to a lonely place by themselves. 33 Now many saw them going, and knew them, and they ran there on foot from all the towns, and got there ahead of them. 34 As he went ashore he saw a great throng, and he had compassion on them, because they were like sheep without a shepherd; and he began to teach them many things. 35 And when it grew late, his disciples came to him and said, "This is a lonely place, and the hour is now late; 36 send them away, to go into the country and villages round about and buy themselves something to eat." 37 But he answered them, "You give them something to eat." And they said to him, "Shall we go and buy two hundred denarii worth of bread, and give it to them to eat?" 38 And he said to them, "How many loaves have you? Go and see." And when they had found out, they said, "Five, and two fish." 39 Then he commanded them all to sit down by companies upon the green grass.	1 After this Jesus went to the other side of the Sea of Galilee, which is the Sea of Tiberias. 2 And a multitude followed him, because they saw the signs which he did on those who were diseased. 3 Jesus went up on the mountain, and there sat down with his disciples. 4 Now the Passover, the feast of the Jews, was at hand. 5 Lifting up his eyes, then, and seeing that a multitude was coming to him, Jesus said to Philip, "How are we to buy bread, so that these people may eat?" 6 This he said to test him, for he himself knew what he would do. 7 Philip answered him, "Two hundred denarii would not buy enough bread for each of them to get a little." 8 One of his disciples, Andrew, Simon Peter's brother, said to him, 9 "There is a lad here who has five barley loaves and two fish; but what are they among so many?" 10 Jesus said, "Make the people sit down." Now there was much grass in the place; so the men sat down, in number about five thousand. 11 Jesus then took the loaves, and when he had given thanks, he distributed them to those who were seated; so also the fish, as much as they wanted. 12 And when they had eaten their fill, he told his disciples, "Gather up the fragments left cont'd.

Mk 6:30–44 cont'd.	Jn 6:1–15 cont'd.
40 So they sat down in groups, by hundreds and by fifties. 41 And taking the five loaves and the two fish he looked up to heaven, and blessed, and broke the loaves, and gave them to the disciples to set before the people; and he divided the two fish among them all. 42 And they all ate and were satisfied. 43 And they took up twelve baskets full of broken pieces and of the fish. 44 And those who ate the loaves were five thousand men.	over, that nothing may be lost." 13 So they gathered them up and filled twelve baskets with fragments from the five barley loaves, left by those who had eaten. 14 When the people saw the sign which he had done, they said, "This is indeed the prophet who is to come into the world!" 15 Perceiving then that they were about to come and take him by force to make him king, Jesus withdrew again to the mountain by himself.

The theological meaning of the miracle is accentuated in preparation for the discourse on the Eucharist, as is the case with other miracles where the miracle is a sign of the teaching that follows it; and light is shed on the personality of Jesus: "he himself knew what he would do" (v. 6). This recalls John 2:25: "because he knew all men and needed no one to bear witness of man; for he himself knew what was in man." Being one with the Father, Jesus has superior knowledge.

This brief overview points to the value of miracles in the life of Jesus and the meaning he wished to give them. The Gospel miracles take on a special coloration in relation to each author's aim in writing in light of particular circumstances and needs of a particular audience. Starting with an unquestionably historical event at the origin of the tradition (for if Christian preaching about Jesus' activity had not been supported by historical fact, it would have been an easy thing to refute it), each Evangelist, guided by the Holy Spirit, recounted miracles that best illustrated the teaching he wished to transmit. In all cases, the miracle narratives make a fundamental point: Jesus worked miracles to confirm the Kingdom's presence in him, to announce the definitive defeat of Satan, and to increase faith in himself. They invite faith and strengthen confidence in him now just as they did at the start.

10

The Preaching of Jesus

Francisco Varo

The most sweeping revisions resulting from historical research concerning Jesus in recent years pertains to his teaching and preaching. Greater familiarity with the teaching of the rabbis in the era of the Second Temple, which corresponds with Jesus' earthly life, and a clearer understanding of how Christ's words and actions fit into the context of Judaism of that period, have made the singularity of his preaching more apparent.

Even a modestly detailed treatment of this subject is impossible here, since it would require several hundred pages. I have provided that elsewhere. Here I limit myself to three topics, with an emphasis on examples, while confining my comments to the comparison of the Gospel texts with other contemporary sources. My topics are the parables, the *halaka* or actualization of the Law, and Jesus' doctrine of God as Father.

1. THE PARABLES

In Jesus' day, preaching in the synagogues during the *Shabbat* was a regular practice (cf. Lk 4:16). The Law of Moses was read weekly, passage by passage, in every community in accord with a plan that called for the entire Pentateuch to be covered every three-and-a-half years.

After the passage of the *Torah* proper to that Sabbath, the *haphtarah*, a text selected from the prophetic books, was read. Then a teacher would undertake to explain the reading and indicate practical ways of carrying out its teaching (cf. Acts 13:15). Often the rabbis used parables—comparisons or examples introduced by saying, "What is this like?" or "With what shall we compare this?" Then came the answer— "This is like," "This can be compared to"—followed by the illustration.

A compilation of rabbinical sayings, *Abot de-Rabbi Nathan*, preserves parables such as this (A. 24):

> As Elisha ben Abuya said: With what can we compare a man who does good deeds and has studied the Torah a lot? With a man who builds first with stones and later with adobe bricks. Even though the water comes pouring down, his building is not destroyed. But with what can we compare a man who does not perform good actions even though he has studied the Torah? With a man who builds first with adobe bricks and then with stone. Even though the flood is not very severe, his whole building soon collapses.

Here, as in all rabbinical parables, we find a striking example, easily remembered, whose lesson one is invited to apply to oneself. The purpose in this instance is to underline the importance of studying the Torah and living it out.

This is the context in which to think of Jesus' preaching. To the simple people of his day, he must—at least at first— have resembled an itinerant teacher similar to many others of the time. He preached in synagogues and in the open air; at city gates, under a tree, in the countryside, on the shores of the lake of Genesareth. His words were entertaining, but was it not surprising that a teacher newly arrived in a village should illustrate his preaching with parables that drew on the familiar formulas and stereotyped themes of rabbinical parables. Yet, if the rabbinical parables are set side by side with his, it is obvious at once that his parables serve to illustrate original teaching.

Like the rabbis, Jesus also taught the Law of Moses. In the Sermon on the Mount, he affirms its value: "Think not that I have come to abolish the law and the prophets; I have come not to abolish them but to fulfill them. For truly, I say to you, till heaven and earth pass away, not an iota, not a dot, will pass from the law until all is accomplished" (Mt 15:17–18).

An example will help make clear the distinctiveness of his teaching in both form and substance. The rabbinical parable quoted above recalls one in the Gospel of St. Matthew (Mt 7:24–27):

> Everyone then who hears these words of mine and does them will be like a wise man who built his house upon the rock; and the rain fell, and the floods came, and the winds blew and beat upon that house, but it did not fall, because it had been founded on the rock. And every one who hears these words of mine and does not do them will be like a foolish man who built his house upon the sand; and the rain fell, and the floods came, and the winds blew and beat against that house, and it fell; and great was the fall of it.

The differences are greater than may appear at first glance. Jesus' words plainly have a vigor lacking in the other parable. The point to be noted here, however, is that in the parable from *Abot de-Rabbi Nathan*, the firm rock was the study and fulfillment of the Law; but for Jesus, the firm rock is not the Torah but the hearing and assimilation of his words. The same literary elements are used in the service of an original teaching.

Sometimes different lessons can be drawn from the same subject. The theme of caring for something that has been entrusted is common to several of Jesus' parables and to well-known rabbinical ones. Christians were careful to pre-serve the parable of the talents (Mt 25:14–30).

> For it will be as when a man going on a journey called his servants and entrusted to them his property; to one he gave five talents, to another two, to another one, to each according to his ability. Then he went away. He who had received the five talents went at once and traded with them; and he made five talents more. So also, he who had the two talents made two talents more. But he who had received the one talent went and dug in the ground and hid his master's money. Now after a long time the master of those servants came and settled accounts with them. And he who had received the five talents came forward, bringing five talents more, saying, "Master, you delivered to me five talents; here I have made five talents more." His master said to him, "Well done, good and faithful servant; you have been faithful over a little, I will set you over much; enter into the joy of your master." And he also who had the two talents came forward, saying, "Master, you delivered to me two talents; here I have made two talents more." His master said to him, "Well done, good and faithful servant; you have been faithful over a little, I will set you over much; enter into the joy of your master." He also who had received the one talent came forward, saying, "Master, I knew you to be a hard man, reaping where you did not sow, and gathering where you did not winnow; so I was afraid, and I went and hid your talent in the ground. Here you have what is yours." But his master answered him, "You wicked and slothful servant! You knew that I reap where I have not sowed, and gather where I have not winnowed? Then you ought to have invested my money with the bankers, and at my coming I should have received what was my own with interest. So take the talent from him, and give it to him who has the ten talents. For to every

one who has will more be given, and he will have abundance; but from him who has not, even what he has will be taken away. And cast the worthless servant into the outer darkness; there men will weep and gnash their teeth."

A similar rabbinical parable was used by Rabbi Eliza to console Rabbi Johanan ben Zakkay when his son died (*Abot de-Rabbi Nathan* A. 14, 3).

> Let me tell you a parable. What is this like? It is like a man with whom a king left on deposit an article of value. Every day this man was worried and said: "Oh my! When will I be free of the responsibility of this deposit?" You too, Master, have had a son versed in the Torah, who studied the Torah, the Prophets and the Writings, Mishna, Halakot, and Hagador. He has now left this world. You should be relieved that you have returned your deposit intact!

Although the theme is fundamentally the same, the rabbinical parable praises keeping in tact what is entrusted, while Jesus' parable is more dynamic. He who merely guards what he receives is reproached and condemned; one who returns twice as much as he receives is praised.

In regard to literary style, Jesus' parables have much more variety and beauty. The protagonists of the rabbinical parables are usually stereotyped: a householder and his servants, a king and his subjects, a householder or king and his children.

Another very important point also deserves mention. Jesus' preaching draws frequently on everyday life to illustrate teaching and shed light on the highest mysteries. In Capernaum, for instance, archeological excavations have shown that the floors of houses were made of rounded, irregular stones. Dirt naturally accumulated in the space between stone and stone, making it very difficult to find a small object that dropped to the ground. Jesus may have had this in mind in Luke 15:8–10:

> Or what woman, having ten silver coins, if she loses one
> coin, does not light a lamp and sweep the house and seek
> diligently until she finds it? And when she has found it, she
> calls together her friends and neighbors, saying, "Rejoice
> with me, for I have found the coin which I had lost." Just
> so, I tell you, there is joy before the angels of God over one
> sinner who repents.

The archaeologist who directed the principal excavations in Capernaum used to joke with his students, "I found the coin which the woman in the parable lost," since careful examination uncovered among the stones and dust coins and other small objects that had been lost by their owners and lain there for centuries.

There are many other examples in the Gospels of our Lord relating his message in tangible ways to his listeners' experience.

2. The *Halaka*

For the people of Galilee Jesus was a teacher whom they enjoyed hearing, both for what he said and for his way of saying it. The chief task of teachers of the Law was to explain the words and the spirit of the *Torah* and teach people to fulfill it in the concrete circumstances of life. This kind of teaching, focusing especially on keeping the commandments, was called *halakica* (from the Hebrew *halaka*, a word derived from the verb *halak*—"to go, to walk"—and meaning something like "path" "or way of conducting oneself").

Almost at the beginning of the public life of Jesus, the Gospel of Matthew presents a great discourse usually referred to as the Sermon on the Mount. An important part of that discourse is devoted to explaining the principal commandments of the *Torah* and how they should be observed (Mt 5:21–48):

> You have heard that it was said to the men of old, "You shall
> not kill; and whoever kills shall be liable to judgment." But

I say to you that every one who is angry with his brother shall be liable to judgment; whoever insults his brother shall be liable to the council, and whoever says, "You fool!" shall be liable to the hell of fire. . . . You have heard that it was said, "You shall not commit adultery." But I say to you that every one who looks at a woman lustfully has already committed adultery with her in his heart.

This is *halakica*. First the text of the Law is cited, then the manner of fulfilling it in keeping with the spirit of the divine commandments is presented. Even the apparent tension between the literal commandment and its more perfect fulfillment was normal in the passionate oral teaching of the rabbis.

Jesus' listeners thus heard a discourse structured in a way familiar to them. Yet in this case the explanations are introduced in an unusual, forceful, and almost provocative manner by the rabbi from Nazareth. Beginning, "You have heard it said . . ." he cites words of the Law which all recognize as having a divine origin and authority, and then he adds: "But I tell you. . . ."

Who is this teacher who dares to correct the Law of Moses? Those familiar with historical-critical analysis of biblical texts agree that it is characteristic of Jesus' style to attribute this interpretative authority to himself. He claims an authority not just equal but superior to that of Moses. No other Jewish teacher makes such a claim.

Only two responses to such a scandalous provocation are possible: This is an arrogant charlatan, albeit a very clever one who speaks to the point and voices ideas in accord with the deepest spirit of the Torah—or this is no less than the Son of God who, through the Torah, teaches the true meaning of God's word.

Perhaps the most daring element of his teaching—expressed in this behavior as well—is Jesus' practice of treating God as Father. His words at the conclusion of the Sermon on the Mount are significant in this regard: "You, therefore, must be perfect, as your heavenly Father is perfect." Thus he points to a theme with resonances in the religious tradition of Israel which nevertheless takes on new meaning and power in his preaching: Not only is God the supreme being, creator and ruler of the world, and considered in this way notably removed from mankind; he also is true Father, who cares for his own with loving affection.

3. The Designation of God as Father

Jesus deals with God as his Father and invites his disciples to do the same. To realize the significance of this attitude we need to begin with questions of context.

The first context is obviously Sacred Scripture—for Jesus, the Old Testament. In the Hebrew Bible the word Father is used to refer to God some fifteen times. He is designated by this name when considered as the creator and, therefore, ruler of the world and of men. But also, and principally, the name has a special connotation when used of his relationship with the people of Israel. God is Father of Israel because he freed the people from slavery in Egypt to make them a holy nation, a people of his own. Serious demands follow on the nation that received such benefits from God's paternal care.

Next there is Judaism in the time of Jesus. It was not common then to refer to God as Father. (In later rabbinic literature, however, the use of "Father" in reference to God does increase slightly, perhaps because a new way of speaking of God was now spreading via formulas analogous to those in the Gospels. In some texts we find invocations that begin *abi(nu) she be-shamayim*—"My (our) Father who is in heaven." But this designation did not become common in Judaism, and is hardly used in the Mishna and the Talmud.)

Most commonly, God is called *Adonai* ("my Lord") or the expression *ha-qadosh baruc hú* ("the Holy One, may he be blessed") is used to substitute for his name. The Targum of the prophets avoids calling God "Father," to the point that circumlocutions in Aramaic are substituted in the few places in the Old Testament where that term is used. And in all cases paternity is attributed to God only in the sense given it by some Old Testament texts, typically that God is Father of the people of Israel. In the very few occasions in which God's fatherhood has reference to his relationship with some individual, the point being made evidently is that God is this person's father because the person is part of Israel and God is Father of Israel.

Thus it is peculiar to Jesus' way of speaking that he calls God Father. In the Gospels, the word "Father" appears more than 170 times on his lips in reference to God, compared with the 15 times it appears in the whole Hebrew Bible, and it has the shades of meaning just discussed. Even the most rigorous historical-critical studies conclude that the designation of God as Father existed in the Tradition before the Gospels were written and was readily accepted by all Christian communities. This could hardly be explained apart from the fact that this is how the historical Jesus spoke of God.

Further confirmation of these conclusions comes from examining the formulas with which, as the Gospel texts uniformly testify, Jesus invoked God. In fact, since the beginning Christian traditions have uniformly agreed that when Jesus prayed to God, he addressed him as Father. Indeed, *whenever* the Evangelists attribute prayers to Jesus, they begin with "Father." The only exception occurs when Jesus, dying on the cross, cries out, "My God, my God, why hast thou forsaken me?" (Mt 27:46; Mk 15:34). Here our Lord spoke the opening words of Psalm 22, which prophesied the death he now was suffering.

Literary and critical analysis indicates that when Jesus addressed God as "Father" he most likely used the Aramaic word *abbá*. His prayer in Gethsemane, moments before the

Passion, is a clear example (cf. Mk 14:36). Jewish prayers never used *abbá* of God, for this was the speech of toddlers: The Aramaic for father was *ab*, to which little ones tended to add "a" much as their counterparts now add "y" to mom and dad in English. All in all, then, for Jesus to speak of God as "Father," and even "Daddy," was profoundly new.

It is also a fact of great importance. To Jewish sensibilities it would have been disrespectful, virtually inconceivable, to address God with so familiar a term as *abbá*. That Jesus dared do so implied something new and unheard of. He spoke with God as a child with his father. In calling God *abbá* he revealed his inmost being in its relationship to God. Moreover, in teaching the "Our Father" to his disciples, he answered them to say as he did: *abbá*. That is to say, he invited them to participate in his filial relationship with God.

4. CONCLUSION

Jesus' teaching expresses a personality so singular that we feel compelled to consider the one who taught this way more than a man. But can we find out who Jesus was from his words? Today in fact it is possible to learn very much about him by studying what he said against the background of what he did and in the context of the preaching of his time. This process leads us to the same conclusion St. Peter reached in reply to Jesus' question at Caesarea Philippi: "But who do you say that I am?" He is someone singularly chosen by God, who teaches and prepares us to receive the grace of God allowing us to confess with Peter: "You are the Christ, the Son of the living God" (Mt 16:16–17). Faith is a gift of God. But reading the Gospels with an open mind is a path given us by the Holy Spirit to attain or strengthen faith.

Bibliography

Here we point to some basic bibliographical material. Each of the books mentioned here will provide more specific bibliographical suggestions.

1. For the chapters: The Critical Path, The Gospels: History and Doctrine, Methodologies, and Some Examples one can find more information in:

Egger, Wilhelm. *How to Read the New Testament: An Introduction to Linguistic and Historical-Critical Methodology*. Peabody, MA: Hendrickson, 1996.

Green, Joel B. (Editor), *Hearing the New Testament: Strategies for Interpretation*. Grand Rapids: W.B. Eerdmans Pub. Co., 1995.

Latourelle, René. *Finding Jesus through the Gospels*. New York: Alba House, 1979.

Neuhaus, Richard John (Editor), *Biblical Interpretation in Crisis: The Ratzinger Conference on Bible and Church*. Grand Rapids: W.B. Eerdmans Pub. Co., 1989.

2. The sections dedicated to the Evangelists could be amplified in:

Hahn, Scott (Editor), *Catholic Bible Dictionary*. New York: Doubleday, 2009.

Senior, Donald (Editor), and John J. Collins (Editor), *The Catholic Study Bible*. New York: Oxford University Press, 2006.

Baker Academic has begun a Catholic commentary on the Gospels and Sacred Scripture with a volume on Mark (Mary Healy, *The Gospel of Mark*, Catholic Commentary on Sacred Scripture. Grand Rapids: Baker Academic, 2008), books covering the rest of the New Testament are scheduled to follow this one.

Liturgical Press, Collegeville, Minn., has completed its *Sacra Pagina Series* on the New Testament. The volumes corresponding to the Gospels are: Daniel J. Harrington, *The Gospel of Matthew*, 1991; John R. Donahue and Daniel J. Harrington, *The Gospel of Mark*, 2002; Luke Timothy Johnson, *The Gospel of Luke*, 1991; Francis J. Moloney, *The Gospel of John*, 1998.

3. The subjects that refer to miracles and the preaching of Jesus can be seen in a more detailed way in treatises of Christology, in some research on the life of Jesus, or in more specialized books. The following might be useful:

Pope Benedict XVI, *Jesus of Nazareth*. New York, NY: Doubleday, 2007.

Gnilka, Joachim, *Jesus of Nazareth: Message and History*. Peabody, MA: Hendrickson, 1997.

Latourelle, René. *The Miracles of Jesus and the Theology of Miracles*. New York: Paulist Press, 1988.

Meyer, Ben F., *The Aims of Jesus*. Princeton Theological Monograph Series 48 (Eugene, OR: Pickwick Publications, 2002).

Ocáriz, Fernando, Lucas F. Mateo-Seco, Jose Antonio Riestra. *The Mystery of Jesus Christ*. Dublin: Four Courts Press, 1994.